Too Young To
Be A Mum

Also by Maggie Hartley:

Tiny Prisoners
Too Scared to Cry
The Little Ghost Girl
A Family for Christmas

Too Young To Be A Mum

CAN JESS LEARN TO BE A GOOD MUMMY,
WHEN SHE IS ONLY A CHILD HERSELF?

MAGGIE HARTLEY

First published in Great Britain in 2017 by Orion Books,
an imprint of The Orion Publishing Group Ltd
Carmelite House, 50 Victoria Embankment,
London EC4Y 0DZ

An Hachette UK company

1 3 5 7 9 10 8 6 4 2

A CIP catalogue record for this book is
available from the British Library.

ISBN (Mass Market Paperback) 978 1 4091 7053 2
ISBN (Export Trade Paperback) 978 1 4091 7052 5

Typeset by Born Group
Printed in Great Britain by CPI Group (UK) Ltd, Croydon CR0 4YY

www.orionbooks.co.uk

Dedication

This book is dedicated to Jess, Darren and Jimmy and all the children and teenagers who have passed through my home. It's been a privilege to have cared for you and to be able to share your stories. And to the children who live with me now. Thank you for your determination, strength and joy and for sharing your lives with me.

Contents

A Message from Maggie

I wanted to write this book to give people an honest account of what it's like to be a foster carer. To talk about some of the challenges that I face on a day-to-day basis and some of the children that I've helped.

My main concern throughout is to protect the children who have been in my care. For this reason, all names and identifying details have been changed, including my own, and no locations have been included. But I can assure you that all my stories are based on real-life cases and are told from my own experiences.

Being a foster carer is a privilege, and I couldn't imagine doing anything else. My house is never quiet, but I wouldn't have it any other way. I hope perhaps my stories will inspire other people to consider fostering, as new carers are always desperately needed.

Maggie Hartley

ONE

On the Move

'Good luck with the unpacking, love. Hope you'll be very happy here.'

The removal men slammed the front door shut, and as I looked around my new living room, my heart sank. Every inch of the dusty carpet was covered with piles of brown cardboard boxes.

I honestly don't know where to start, I thought as I flopped down onto my settee that was still wrapped in protective plastic.

Just to add insult to injury, I didn't know where the kettle was so I couldn't even make myself a cup of tea. I desperately needed a cuppa after the stressful day I'd had. We'd just moved house, and while I was in despair about the state of the place and all the unpacking I had to do, my long-term foster placements Lily and Louisa were practically bouncing off the walls with excitement.

'It's massive!' shouted Louisa, running down the stairs. 'My bedroom is double the size of my old one.'

'And have you seen the garden?' Lily grinned. 'Maggie, can we get a trampoline?'

'Let me at least unpack this lot first before we start thinking about trampolines,' I told her.

We'd only moved about ten miles from our old house, but the way the boundaries fell, it meant we were now living in a new county. The old place had been a four-bed terrace with a postage-stamp-sized garden. So when this house had come up for the same price that I'd been able to sell my old one for, I'd jumped at the chance to move.

It was a detached Victorian house, and although it didn't look that huge from the outside, it had six bedrooms spread over three floors. There was also a playroom at the back and a big garden. I knew it was a home that I'd never grow out of, and even though I was going to use one spare bedroom as an office, it meant I still had two more that I could use especially for fostering. The area was a bit quieter and greener than our previous neighbourhood, and I was closer to my good friends Anne and Vicky who were fellow foster carers.

It was still close enough for Lily, seven, to keep on going to the same school, and for seventeen-year-old Louisa to carry on her nursery nursing course at college. However, the move did signify a big change for me in terms of my fostering. Ever since I'd started fostering I'd always worked for the local authority, but now that we'd moved, I'd decided to join a fostering agency. Both Anne and Vicky worked for the same agency and they'd recommended it to me. It was something that I'd been thinking about for a while. You seemed to get a bit more support and continuity if you worked for an agency. I was already on my fifth supervising social worker this year with the local authority, and staff were continually leaving and being moved around. Also, an agency offered you a lot more training. Foster carers were often put off joining an agency as you tended to get the more challenging cases. A local authority would offer a child to its own carers first, and if there was no one suitable then they would offer the placement out to an agency – therefore you tended to get the children no one else wanted. It made me feel sad, as these were the kind of kids who needed love and a stable home life more than anything, so I had no qualms about taking on a child who had been deemed difficult. Even when I had worked for the local authority, I thrived on challenging cases. Every child came with their own issues – I believed it was more about how you as a carer reacted to them.

My one worry about resigning from the local authority was that they wouldn't give me permission to keep on fostering Lily and Louisa, so it was such a relief when they said I could. I'd had them for coming up to four years, and we were a tight little family unit.

I was proud of how both girls had turned out despite everything they'd been through in the past. Lily had been taken into care because her father was an alcoholic and violent to her mother, who refused to leave him. Lily looked like an angel with her big blue eyes and golden ringlets, but her behaviour had certainly been a challenge at first. She had incredible temper tantrums, threw toys and smashed things. But after living with me for a few months, she'd gradually started to calm down. She was still a lively, boisterous little thing, but she was doing well at school and had a lovely kind nature. Despite everything that had happened, she had a good relationship with her mum, Jane, and saw her every week for a couple of hours at a contact centre.

Louisa had come to me at around the same time as Lily after her parents were tragically killed in a car crash. Alone and struggling to cope with her grief, she was painfully shy at first, but she had turned into a strong, confident, determined young woman who wanted to be a nanny. She'd shot up over the past few months, so she was taller than me now, and with her sleek brown bob and carefully applied make-up, she looked so grown-up and sophisticated these days. This house was going to be a fresh start for all of us.

'God only knows what my new supervising social worker's going to think of the state of this place when she comes round tomorrow,' I sighed.

It had taken months for me to move to the agency. I'd had meetings, provided references, they'd talked to the local authority and read through my file. Finally I'd gone in front of a panel, and thankfully I'd been approved.

'Why on earth did you invite her round the day after we moved?' said Louisa. 'You must be mad.'

Louisa didn't mince her words, and I could always rely on her to tell it like it was.

'It seemed like a good idea at the time and it needed to be done at some point,' I told her.

Becky was coming round to do a health and safety assessment of the new house, to check that it was safe for any children who came to live here. She'd be looking at the bedroom space, checking that we had things like smoke alarms fitted, a fire extinguisher and a first aid box.

I had less than twenty-four hours to try and get everything sorted, or at least clear some of the boxes so it didn't look too chaotic. As a single carer who had never been married, I relied on the support of my friends, and luckily I had a great group of people around me. We'd only been at the new house for an hour when Anne and her husband Bob turned up to help.

When Anne walked in and saw the state of the place, she laughed.

'Oh, Maggie,' she sighed, 'I know how much you hate clutter. I bet you're going out of your mind.'

'I'm itching to get it all unpacked,' I said.

While I began going through some of the boxes downstairs, she and Bob went upstairs and started putting the beds together and moving furniture into the correct places. Three hours later, we were all dead on our feet. Bob nipped out for fish and chips and we sat round in the living room eating them out of the wrappers as our kitchen table hadn't been reassembled yet.

'I love this house,' sighed Lily, licking salt and vinegar off her greasy fingers. 'I think we're all going to be very happy here.' I totally agreed.

Thanks to Anne and Bob, we had somewhere to sleep and eventually the girls went off to bed while I stayed up half the night unpacking more boxes.

The next morning at 10 a.m on the dot, there was a sharp knock at the door. It was my new supervising social worker, Becky, the person who had interviewed me to see if I was suitable to join the agency. She seemed like a nice woman, but I was still nervous. Becky was very tall, in fact she towered over me, and she was enthusiastic and bubbly. She had two children of her own and from my first impressions, she had a good understanding of kids and their needs.

'Wow,' she said, looking around. 'It looks like you've lived here for months, never mind less than twenty-four hours.'

'We're getting there,' I told her. 'You should have seen it yesterday.'

I gave her a quick tour.

'It's a lovely big house,' she said.

'Even though it might look like I'm sorted, I don't want to take any placements on for at least a week so I can make sure I'm properly unpacked,' I told her.

'That's no problem,' she said. 'From my perspective, everything meets regulations and the bedrooms look ready for a placement to move in, so just give me a shout when you feel ready.'

After a week of hard graft, the last box was emptied and the house started to feel like home. When Vicky popped in, she was shocked.

'Blimey, it's like a different place,' she said.

'I've literally not stopped,' I said. 'But we've done it.'

There were things I wanted to do, in time, like paint the rooms and knock through the kitchen and dining room, but for now we were as good as sorted.

'I'm going to phone the agency later today and put myself on the available list,' I told her.

'I bet all your lovely new bedrooms will soon be full,' she said.

Some foster carers don't like the sense of the unknown you have between placements, but I quite like the anticipation of not knowing when the phone is going to ring and when the next child is going to arrive – or children. My experience with the local authority over the years was that I was only ever free for a few days at most between placements, and sometimes even hours. But I wasn't sure what to expect now that I worked for an agency.

As it happened, the call came one morning, four days later. I'd just got in from driving Lily to school, which took a bit longer these days.

'Maggie, it's Becky from the agency,' said a voice. 'We've just had a referral for a placement and I wondered if you'd be interested?'

'Yes, of course,' I said. 'Tell me more.'

'I would if I could, but I'm afraid I don't have a lot of information at this stage. All I know is that it's a three-day-old boy and potentially his sixteen-year-old mother as well.'

'Wow, that's a tiny baby,' I said. 'I love newborns, and I'm happy to help.'

I'd done mother-and-baby placements before and had really enjoyed them. People always make assumptions that young mums can't parent, but I liked proving them wrong.

'Where are they coming from?' I asked.

Becky explained that the police had been called to a disturbance on an estate last night between a group of family members. The family was known to the police and had a long history of drug and alcohol abuse and petty crime.

'At the address was a sixteen-year-old girl who wasn't related to anyone there and her newborn son. The officers were concerned that a baby so young was living in this unsuitable environment, so they contacted Social Services.

'The emergency duty team is going out to the address this morning so we'll keep you posted. Obviously with a baby that age Social Services would prefer to try and keep him with his mum, but if the girl won't come into care voluntarily then they'll have to issue an Emergency Protection Order on the baby.'

'No problem, I'll wait to hear,' I said.

I spent the rest of the day nursing my mobile phone while I dug out a baby monitor and a few newborn Babygros that I had in my spare stash. I'd got plenty of nappies left over from previous placements but they were for older babies, so I quickly nipped out to the supermarket to stock up on nappies, tins of formula and cotton wool so I was all prepared. I'd asked one of Lily's friends' mums to bring her home from school as I wanted to stay in just in case Social Services turned up without warning. But by the time both girls were home, I still hadn't heard a thing.

'We've hopefully got a new placement arriving later on,' I told them. 'It's a three-day-old baby.'

Lily was beside herself with excitement at the idea of such a tiny baby coming to live with us.

'They don't do much, you know, Lils, at that age,' Louisa told her. 'They can't play or anything, they just lie there.'

Ever since she'd started her childcare course, Louisa thought she was the fountain of all knowledge when it came to babies and toddlers.

'Well, I can just cuddle it,' said Lily. 'I bet it's cute.'

'It's a "he", not an "it",' I told her. 'And you have to be very gentle with newborns. His mummy might be coming with him too.'

'Who's its mum?' she asked.

'I don't honestly know, love,' I told her. 'I don't know anything about her yet. I don't even know that they're definitely coming.'

At 5.30 p.m. Becky rang back.

'Sorry about the delay, Maggie,' she said. 'Social Services have just called. They're still at the house talking to the girl, but they think they've persuaded her to come into care voluntarily with the baby. They should be with you in the next couple of hours.'

'Good,' I said. 'A baby as young as that needs to be with its mum.'

It was gone 8 p.m. when the doorbell finally rang. It was late September and the nights had quickly started to draw in so I flicked the porch light on as I went to answer it. As I opened the door, I felt the usual mix of nerves and anticipation that I always had when a new child was arriving. A woman was standing on the doorstep. She could only have been in her late forties but she was dressed like an old-fashioned schoolmistress in a checked A-line skirt, a grey woollen jumper and sensible flat shoes.

'Hello,' I said brightly. 'I'm Maggie. Good to meet you.'

'I'm Katherine Hargreaves, the social worker,' she said, shaking my hand in a very brusque and businesslike manner. 'And this is Jess and baby James.'

Katherine was a rather large woman who seemed to fill the whole doorstep with her bulk, and to be honest I couldn't see anyone else with her.

'I keep telling you his name's Jimmy, not James,' said an exasperated voice from behind her.

'Oh yes, my apologies,' said Katherine. 'Baby Jimmy.'

'Please come in,' I said.

When Katherine moved out of the way I could finally see Jess for myself. She stared back at me with big, frightened blue eyes. She looked like a little girl, never mind sixteen, and she was very small with short, bleached-blonde hair. I was reminded that the poor girl had only given birth three days ago by her stomach, which was still distended. She was wearing a fitted T-shirt and tight jeans that must have been uncomfortable for her swollen, post-birth body and she looked exhausted. Fast asleep in her arms, tightly wrapped in a blanket, was the tiniest baby I'd seen in a long time. He was small but absolutely perfect, with little rosebud lips and a shock of dark hair.

Louisa, who'd been watching TV in the living room, came out to say hello.

'This is Louisa,' I told her. 'I'm afraid Lily's already in bed, but you'll meet her in the morning.'

'Hi,' said Louisa, going over and taking a peep at Jimmy. 'He's a lovely baby.'

'Ta,' said Jess.

Lily, who was supposed to be asleep, had obviously heard the door go and couldn't resist coming down for a peep.

'Hello,' she said shyly. 'I'm Lily.'

'Hi,' said Jess, giving her a weak smile.

'Maggie, is this the baby that's coming to live with us?' Lily asked.
I nodded.

'Yes, this is Jimmy and his mummy Jess,' I told her. 'Now get yourself back into bed. You're going to be shattered for school tomorrow.'

Lily quickly scampered back up the stairs.

'Do you want me to hold Jimmy while you go and bring in your things?' Katherine asked Jess in her loud, sing-song voice.

'It's OK,' I said, 'I'll get them for her.'

All Jess had with her was a small rucksack and a cheap, flimsy buggy that looked like it had seen better days.

'As you can see, she hasn't got much,' said Katherine.

She was like a bossy schoolmistress, and I could tell from the way Jess rolled her eyes whenever Katherine spoke that there was no love lost between them. I could practically feel the tension in the air.

'Come through to the kitchen,' I said. 'Would you like a drink or something to eat?'

'No, thank you,' said Jess politely.

She seemed very meek and mild, but I could tell from the way she dragged her feet that she didn't want to be here.

'Maggie, shall you and I sort out the paperwork?' said Katherine efficiently.

'Jess, do you want to take Jimmy and have a sit-down with Louisa in the front room, and then I'll show you your bedroom in a bit,' I told her.

She shrugged but did what I'd asked.

Katherine bustled through to the kitchen where she produced the relevant forms for me to sign.

'Is there anything you can tell me about the case?' I asked.

She explained that rather than Social Services take Jimmy into care, Jess had agreed to come into care herself under a Section 20, which meant that she could stay with her baby.

'Because she's sixteen, Jess is free to come and go as she pleases during the day but she's been told that she must sleep here. The main aim for you is to assess her parenting skills and help her get the baby into a good routine.'

'And can you tell me anything about where Jess has come from?' I asked. 'Why is she in the care system?'

Katherine sighed and looked at her watch.

'There's a placement meeting here at nine tomorrow. It's getting late now, so if you don't mind I'll save all the long-winded explanations for then. I'll only have to repeat it all to your supervising social worker.'

I was starting to see where Jess was coming from. Katherine's manner made me bristle too.

'Right then, Maggie, I'll see you in the morning,' she said.

As she walked past the living room, she called out to Jess.

'Bye, Jess. Sleep well.'

Jess gave her a look that could only be described as one of contempt.

After I'd shown Katherine out, I went in to see her. She was sat on the sofa, Jimmy still contentedly asleep in her arms

'You must be exhausted,' I said. 'I bet it's been a long, emotional day for you.'

'Put it this way, it's not been my best day,' she sighed.

I smiled sympathetically. At least I could offer her a warm, safe place to be with her baby after all the drama of the last twenty-four hours.

'Let me show you your bedroom,' I said.

I took her rucksack and led her upstairs.

'We've only recently moved into this house, so this room isn't how I'd choose to decorate it but it's clean and hopefully comfortable,' I told her.

The woodchip walls were painted a bright lilac and the Artex ceiling was a dull cream colour. There was a double bed, and I'd put a Moses basket and a cot in there so she could choose whichever she preferred Jimmy to sleep in.

I suspected from the size of her rucksack that she hadn't got much, so I showed her the chest of drawers with the Babygros and vests in them.

'I know tiny babies can go through several outfits a day.' I smiled. 'So there's lots of spare clothes in there if you need them.

'Did you bring any nappies?' I asked her.

'Just a couple,' said Jess, so I was pleased I'd been to the supermarket and stocked up on supplies.

'What about bottles?' I asked. 'Or are you breastfeeding?'

'No, he's just having bottles but I'm fine,' she said, pulling out a grubby bottle from her rucksack. I suspected that was her only one.

'I'll put it in the steriliser so it'll be ready for Jimmy's next feed.'

'What about formula?'

'I've got a carton,' she said.

'When that runs out I've got a couple of tins of formula downstairs, so help yourself.'

I made a mental note to go to the supermarket after the planning meeting in the morning and pick up some more bottles.

I showed her the bathroom in case she wanted to have a bath, and I also pointed out where my bedroom was.

'If you need anything at all, even if it's the middle of the night, then give me a knock,' I said. 'I'll leave Jimmy's bottle and the formula downstairs in the kitchen.'

'OK, thanks,' she said. 'He's just had a feed so he won't need one till later.'

'Have you got everything you need?' I asked her.

Jess shrugged and looked like she was about to burst into tears.

'What is it?' I asked. 'Is there anything I can do?'

'No offence or nothing, but I really don't want to be here,' she said.

'I'm sorry,' I told her. 'But hopefully you'll feel a bit more comfortable when you've settled in.'

'I won't,' she said firmly. 'I won't be settling in cos I don't want to be here. I want to be with Darren.'

I had no idea who Darren was, but Jess looked so upset and tired I didn't have the heart to ask her. Maybe Katherine had been right after all. It was getting late and perhaps some things could wait until the morning.

TWO

Pushing the Boundaries

Jess was in bed by 9 p.m., and after that I didn't hear a thing from either her or the baby. I'd heard her in the shower before bed and while she was in the bathroom, I'd poked my head round her bedroom door to check on Jimmy and seen that he was fast asleep in the cot, which reassured me. I sterilised her bottle as I'd promised and left it downstairs along with some formula for when she needed to feed him in the night.

At midnight I decided to admit defeat and go to bed, but although everything was quiet, I couldn't settle. I was always like this on the first night of a placement, and it took me a few days to get used to the fact that there was someone new in the house. My mind was working overtime thinking about Jess and everything she'd been through in the past twenty-four hours, and wondering if Jimmy was OK. At least when it was a younger child I could go into their bedroom and check on them, but I couldn't do that with a sixteen-year-old. Her door was firmly closed and I had to respect her privacy.

I walked past her bedroom two or three times in the early hours of the morning and stopped to see if I could hear any noise, but there wasn't a peep. I hadn't even heard Jimmy crying, which was unusual as newborn babies weren't known for being quiet. It was a long, restless night and I dozed on and off.

At 5 a.m. I gave up hope of ever going back to sleep and went downstairs in the dark to make a cup of tea. My heart sank when I turned on the kitchen light and saw that the sterilised bottle was still on the side with the unused carton of formula. Newborns like Jimmy needed feeding every few hours, even during the night, otherwise there was a risk they'd become severely dehydrated.

Ten minutes later I heard footsteps padding down the stairs and Jess came into the kitchen. She was wearing the same top and jeans from the day before and I wondered if she'd bothered to put on the pyjamas I'd left out for her. Thankfully Jimmy seemed OK. He was wriggling around in Jess's arms, and I was relieved when he let out an almighty cry.

'I think someone's hungry,' I said. 'I'll hold him if you want, while you make up a bottle.'

'Ta,' she said, passing him to me.

I didn't want to go in all guns blazing and tell her off about the bottle. My aim was to try and build up her confidence in her parenting abilities, not destroy it.

'Did you sleep well?' I asked as she gave the carton a shake and poured out the milk.

I couldn't help but notice that she hadn't washed her hands.

'OK I suppose,' she sighed.

'I didn't hear Jimmy in the night,' I mentioned casually. 'Did he not wake up wanting a bottle?'

'No.' She smiled. 'He's a good sleeper for a little 'un, ain't he?'

I was amazed that he'd actually slept through and hadn't been screaming the house down like he was now. When the bottle was ready and warmed, Jess sat down and I passed Jimmy to her. His mouth latched onto the teat straight away and he guzzled hungrily. The poor little mite was starving.

'Jess,' I said gently, 'you know that babies Jimmy's age need feeding every three to four hours even in the night, otherwise they can get very poorly. Normally they wake you up and let you know they're hungry, but if they don't then you need to make sure that you wake up and give them a feed anyway.'

'Well, I gave him one last night,' she said.

'That's still way too long for a newborn to go without milk,' I told her. 'The danger is they get lethargic and then they don't have the energy to feed, so they go downhill very quickly.'

'How am I meant to know?' she huffed. 'No one bloody told me.'

'Hasn't the midwife been to see you since you came out of hospital?' I asked. 'You and Jimmy should be having daily checks.'

'I think she came round the first day but I was out at McDonald's,' she said.

I made a mental note to discuss the midwife's visits at the placement meeting later. I could tell that I'd really worried Jess.

'Do you think he'll be all right?' she asked, looking concerned. 'Will he get poorly? He won't die, will he?'

'He looks fine to me,' I said. 'As long as he's alert and his nappies are wet, then you know he's OK. You've just got to make sure that from now on he has regular feeds.'

I felt sorry for Jess. How was she supposed to know how to look after her baby if no one had taken the time to show her?

'I'll make sure Katherine or I get in touch with the community midwife so she knows you've changed address and she can come round here and check both you and Jimmy. You only gave birth a few days ago. You need to look after yourself.'

Jimmy had gulped his bottle down at record speed.

'Has anyone shown you how to wind him?' I asked.

I could tell by the puzzled look on Jess's face that she hadn't got a clue what I was talking about.

'It's to help him bring up any air he's taken in when he was having a feed,' I explained, putting him over my shoulder. 'If you pat his back gently like this then he'll have a good burp.

'I don't mind doing it if you want to go upstairs and have a shower,' I told her. 'And if you need anything washing, then let me know and I'll put it in the machine for you.'

I was mindful of the fact that she'd hardly got anything with her.

'OK,' she said.

'By the way, did Katherine tell you yesterday that there's a placement meeting happening here at 9 a.m.?' I said.

'No,' said Jess. 'What's that?'

'It will just be us and my supervising social worker Becky and Katherine, and we'll be talking about you and how we can help you.'

Jess's face fell.

'That Katherine's coming again?' she sighed. 'She was only round 'ere yesterday.'

'Well, she is your social worker,' I said. 'And it's important that she knows what you want.'

'She ain't bothered about what I want,' said Jess. 'And I know exactly what *she* wants. She wants me and Darren to split up and she wants to take Jimmy off me. I know it.'

'Jess, I'm really sorry but I don't even know who Darren is. Is he your boyfriend?' I asked.

She nodded sadly.

'Me and Jimmy were living at his place when they came and took us,' she sighed, her big blue eyes filling up with tears.

'I can see you're upset, but we'll talk about all of this at the meeting later. That's why it's important that you're there. It's about you and your future.'

'There's no point,' she sighed. 'That bitch has already decided that I'm not good enough to be a mum.'

'Honestly, that isn't the case,' I pleaded. 'All we want to do is help you and make sure you and Jimmy are safe.'

However, my words fell on deaf ears and Jess stormed off upstairs. Poor girl, I could see she felt as if the world was against her.

I glanced down at Jimmy nestled into the crook of my arm. It was the first time that I'd managed to have a proper look at him. He was in the same grubby Babygro that he'd arrived in the night before, but his nappy had been changed and his skin seemed clean. After years of experience working with badly neglected babies and toddlers, I could tell even with a baby that young if they'd been subjected to trauma, and I could see that he was well cared for and content. When I held him he nestled into me – he wasn't jumpy or restless and he seemed very settled.

'You're a beauty, aren't you,' I said, stroking his tiny hand.

He had perfect porcelain skin and dark brown hair that stuck up in wispy tufts. He nodded off in my arms, so I brought the Moses basket down from upstairs and settled him in that before the girls got up and I made them breakfast.

'Hello, Baby Jimmy,' said Lily when she came downstairs.

'Don't wake him, lovely, he's having a little sleep,' I told her. 'Jess is having a shower but she should be down shortly.'

But by the time Jess reappeared, both Lily and Louisa had left for the day.

Just before 9 a.m. Katherine arrived. 'Morning, Jess,' she said as she breezed through the front door. 'How are you today?'

'Not great,' she scowled. 'I'd be a lot better if I was at Darren's.'

Katherine chose to ignore her comment and bustled into the living room.

'Let's go in here, shall we?'

Becky arrived shortly afterwards, and I made everyone a cup of tea before we all sat down. Jess made it clear she didn't want to be there and was doing lots of huffing and puffing.

'So how are you feeling today?' Katherine asked her.

'Not very happy at all,' she said.

'Oh dear, what is it? Is there a problem with Maggie, or is it the house you're not happy with?'

Thanks very much, Katherine, I thought to myself.

'No,' said Jess. 'She's really nice and the house is really nice. I've told you, I don't want to be here.'

'We went through all this yesterday,' said Katherine. 'If you want to be with Jimmy then you have to be here. If you'd stayed at Darren's, then we would have had to take the baby away from you and put him into care.'

'I don't see why,' said Jess, her eyes filling up with tears. 'The three of us should be allowed to be together.'

She sat there with her arms folded defensively while the rest of us carried on our discussion.

'I was saying to Jess this morning that it's very important she sees a midwife,' I said.

'Most definitely,' said Katherine. 'I phoned yesterday and gave them your new address, and they said a community midwife should be able to pop round here sometime this afternoon.'

'I ain't waiting around for no midwife,' said Jess. 'In fact, I'm fed up of this. It's boring. I'm going out.'

With that she stood up, plucked Jimmy out of the Moses basket and walked into the hallway.

I jumped up and went after her.

'Where are you going, Jess?' I asked.

'Darren's,' she said.

'You really should be here for this meeting,' I urged her. 'It's all about your and Jimmy's future.'

'It's pointless,' she sighed. 'No one's listening to what I want anyway.'

'Well, if you won't stay for the meeting, at least wait to see the midwife,' I told her. 'It's important that she checks Jimmy and makes sure he's feeding well and that you're OK after the birth.'

'He's fine,' she said. 'And I'll be fine as long as I can see Darren. I ain't staying here, I'm going.'

I could see her mind was made up and that there was no point arguing with her. It wasn't as if I could physically stop her from leaving the house.

'What time will you be back?'

'Dunno.' She shrugged. 'Tonight. Probably eleven.'

'That's very late to be out with such a little baby,' I said. 'How about nine at the very latest?'

'All right.' She tutted.

'Has Katherine said that it's OK for you to go to Darren's house?'

'Go and ask her yourself,' she told me. 'She only said I had to sleep here. She didn't say nothing about the daytime.'

I watched as Jess struggled to put up the buggy that she'd brought with her. It was a rusty metal frame with a flimsy bit of material for the seat and it looked like it was about to fall apart.

'Jess, you can't put Jimmy in that,' I told her.

'Why not?' she said. 'I've been padding it out with a blanket and my denim jacket and he's been all right.'

'Newborns need to lie flat and be properly supported. It doesn't recline and he could fall out of that.'

'Well, Darren's mum gave it to me. I couldn't afford to buy one.'

'Wait here,' I said. 'I've got a buggy in the understairs cupboard you can borrow.'

It was a pushchair with a pram attachment that would be much more suitable for a newborn.

'How are you going to get there?' I said.

'Dunno.' She shrugged. 'A bus into town and a bus to Darren's.'

'Be careful,' I said. 'Have you got bottles for Jimmy and clean nappies?'

She shook her head. I went and got a pile of nappies, some cartons of formula and a bottle and put them in a carrier bag for her.

'Oh, and here's a blanket and a cardigan for him,' I said. 'He'll be too cold in just a Babygro. I know it's only September but it can be quite chilly in the mornings.'

'Ta,' she said before opening the front door and going out.

I went back into the living room where Katherine and Becky were waiting.

'She's gone to Darren's,' I told them.

'Who's Darren?' asked Becky.

'Her boyfriend,' said Katherine. 'That's whose house we picked her up from yesterday.'

'Is he Jimmy's father?' asked Becky and Katherine nodded.

'She seems very devoted to him,' I said. 'How long have they been together?'

'Since Jess was twelve,' said Katherine. 'But it's just puppy love. It won't last.'

'What makes you so sure?' I asked. 'Four years is a long time to be together at that age.'

'They're enjoying playing mummies and daddies at the minute, but once the novelty wears off and the reality of caring for a newborn kicks in, I bet we won't see him for dust,' she scoffed.

I thought she was being very dismissive. It was an unusual situation for me, as all of the teenage mothers I'd fostered in the past had been single parents and not part of a couple.

'So why did she have to leave Darren's and come into care?' asked Becky.

Katherine sighed. 'I've had the pleasure, if you could call it that, of being involved with Darren's family on and off over the years.'

She explained that Darren was seventeen and had three older brothers, all of whom had been in and out of the care system.

'Mum has an alcohol problem,' she said. 'The family were part of the travelling community, although they've now got a council house.

'The boys caused so much trouble in the care system they eventually went back to mum. All of them now live at home,

22

so there are five of them crammed into a three-bedroom house.

'They often get members of the travelling community turning up, so there are caravans outside and bonfires in the front garden. The police are there practically every week and the boys have been in and out of prison. There's a lot of buying and selling of stolen goods, stolen cars, fights and drug dealing.

'The house itself is chaotic and not very clean, and there are always people coming and going. Jess and Darren were squeezed into a tiny box room and sharing a single bed with Jimmy, which I didn't think was safe. Believe me, it's no place for a newborn baby to live.'

'It doesn't sound like it,' I sighed.

'What about Jess's parents?' I said. 'Couldn't she stay with them?'

Katherine shook her head.

'It's a similar story, unfortunately. Jess is the only child of a single mum. Mum's a drug addict and a prostitute. Jess has been in and out of care all her life but as she got older, she returned to mum and was just about able to fend for herself.

'Mum doesn't like Darren's family, and when Jess found out she was pregnant at fifteen, she washed her hands of her. I think her exact words were that she'd been on the game for years and not managed to get knocked up, and Jess was a stupid f***ing slag.'

'She sounds pleasant,' said Becky.

'Unfortunately Jess slipped off the radar. She hasn't been to school for months, however the school thought Social Services were aware of it but there was a change of workers and they weren't. We didn't know that she was pregnant. She told the midwives that she was living at home with mum, so there was no cause for concern.'

My heart went out to these two vulnerable young people. Of course they didn't know how to be good parents because neither of them had had good parenting themselves, by the sound of it.

However, that didn't mean they could never be. Jess had only been with me a few hours, but I could tell by the way she was with Jimmy that she loved her baby.

'If you don't mind me asking, Katherine, what's the aim of this placement?' said Becky. 'Wasn't Jess removed from Darren's house yesterday because it was considered to be an unsuitable place for a baby? Yet you're happy for her to spend most of the day there.'

Katherine sighed. 'We had to start somewhere, and the only way I could persuade her to come into care voluntarily was to say that she only had to sleep here.

'Unfortunately because she's just turned sixteen we can't physically stop her going to Darren's, but over the next few days let's try and do all we can to keep her at this house more. I'm hoping that once she gets used to being here she'll realise things are a lot more comfortable than at Darren's.

'Maggie, you need to make sure that she's here for midwife appointments and explain that she needs to be here more so that you can help her get the baby into a proper routine.'

'So, like Becky asked, what is the aim of the placement?' I said.

'We want you to keep a close eye on Jess and assess her parenting skills,' said Katherine. 'She hasn't got any siblings and hasn't grown up around young children and, as we know, she hasn't exactly got a great mothering role model.

'I want to check that she's providing Jimmy with a decent standard of care and that he's not in danger.'

'From what I've seen so far, she clearly loves her son,' I said. 'A lot of mother-and-baby placements are more about giving the mum confidence in her own abilities.'

'I think it's more about making sure that Jimmy isn't at risk of being harmed,' replied Katherine. 'Jess doesn't seem to have a clue about the basics. Look at that flimsy buggy she's been pushing him around in.'

'But she can learn,' I said.

'Well, you can try,' said Katherine. 'However, I suspect long-term we're probably going to be looking at adoption. It might be the better option for everyone.'

In my opinion it was way too soon to be talking about adoption. Jimmy was three days old, for God's sake – we couldn't write off Jess's ability to be a good parent at this early stage. I felt Katherine was being very dismissive of both Jess's abilities as a mum and her relationship with Darren.

I started to realise that this placement was going to be a challenge. Katherine seemed to be against Jess and Darren based on her past involvement with their families, and I felt sad that she wasn't giving them a chance to prove themselves. They weren't their parents, and they should be judged as individuals.

Jess was sixteen now, and no matter what Katherine said I couldn't physically keep her in the house and stop her from going to Darren's if she wanted to. I didn't even know if she was going to come back tonight. All I could do was wait and hope that she and Jimmy were safe and would turn up later.

THREE

Broken Promises

Checking the clock on the wall for the umpteenth time, I paced up and down the kitchen.

Where the heck was she?

I'd told Jess to be back at nine, but it was 9.45 p.m. and there was no sign of her and Jimmy.

'I'm going to bed now,' said Louisa.

'OK, love,' I told her. 'Sleep well.'

'I hope she comes back soon.'

'Me too,' I sighed.

I was so frustrated with Jess, as I knew it wasn't going to do her any favours being late in on her second night with me. I'd have to record it in my notes that I emailed to the agency every evening – information that would be passed on to Katherine. It would be another mark against Jess's name as far as she was concerned, and it was only going to give her more ammunition to prove that she wasn't a fit mother for Jimmy.

I only hoped Jess was at Darren's like she'd told me, but I couldn't help feeling a little prickle of worry when I thought of a newborn baby being out there in the dark and on public transport so late.

Time ticked on. I emptied the dishwasher and packed Lily's school bag for the following day, but there was still no sign of Jess and Jimmy. When it got to 10 p.m. I decided to go and have a look out of the living room window. Much to my relief, just as I pushed the curtain back a car pulled up outside and I saw Jess get out of the front seat with Jimmy fast asleep in her arms.

I opened the door before she had a chance to knock, as I didn't want to wake the girls.

'You're late,' I told her. 'You agreed to be back at nine and it's gone ten now.'

'Oh, is it?' she said. 'Sorry, I lost track of time.'

'That's not good enough. You have to be back at the agreed time,' I said. 'I was about to call the police.'

'Why would you do that?' she huffed. 'You knew I was at Darren's.'

'That's what I have to do,' I told her. 'It's procedure. If you're not back at the set time then I have a duty to report you as missing.'

Any child under eighteen in the care system is considered vulnerable, and if they don't turn up at the allotted time it is a foster carer's responsibility to report them missing. Then it is up to the police to judge how urgent a case it is.

'Even though you're back now, I'll have to record the fact that you're an hour late in my notes and Katherine will need to be informed.'

'Why are you grassing me up to her?' wailed Jess. 'It ain't fair. You knew where I was. I'd just forgotten about the time.'

'I've got to, Jess, it's my job,' I said. 'You've only been with me twenty-four hours. I didn't know for sure where you were.

You don't have a phone, so I couldn't ring you, and for all I know you could have been having problems with the buses.'

'Well, I wasn't,' said Jess. 'Darren dropped me back.'

'Oh, so he has a car then?' I asked.

'Er, no, actually it was his mate who dropped me back,' she said hesitantly.

'And, Jess, if you're going in a car you really need to put Jimmy in a car seat,' I told her. 'It's not safe for him just to be on your knee.'

'I had the seat belt on,' she said. 'Anyway, I ain't got a car seat. I couldn't afford one.'

'You should have told me,' I replied. 'I've got one you can have that attaches to the base of the pram. I'll get it out for you tomorrow.'

'OK,' she sighed.

Jess suddenly looked very tired and I felt guilty for being so hard on her. She'd only given birth four days ago, and since then she'd been uprooted from her boyfriend's house and, in Jess's words, forced into care.

'Have you had anything to eat?' I asked. 'Do you want a sandwich or a cup of tea? I've made Jimmy a bottle up in case he's due a feed.'

'No, ta,' she said. 'I think I'll get off to bed.'

'By the way, before you go,' I said, calling after her, 'Katherine's arranged for the midwife to come round at ten tomorrow morning and it's really important that you're here.'

'OK,' she sighed. 'I've got the message.'

I was so exasperated with her. She didn't seem to realise how important it was to obey the rules and to be seen to be co-operating with Social Services. She wasn't seeing the bigger picture or understanding the consequences of her actions. If she continued to push the boundaries, then it would only force Katherine into issuing a care order on Jimmy and starting the adoption process.

Before I went to bed, I finished off my email to the agency. *Jess was an hour late back to the placement tonight*, I wrote. *I don't know whether she was pushing me or just testing the boundaries, or whether she genuinely had lost track of time and didn't realise how important it was to be back promptly.*

I knew we'd need to have another chat about it the following day.

The midwife came round the next morning and examined Jimmy.

'He's putting on weight nicely.' She smiled. 'You've got a happy, healthy little boy there.'

'Well done,' I told Jess, and I could tell by her little smile that she was really pleased.

As the midwife was leaving, Katherine rang.

'I've just spoken to Becky about last night's events,' she said. 'I'll pop round in an hour or so and have a talk to Jess. Is that OK?'

'Yes, that's fine,' I said.

I put the phone down and went to tell Jess what was happening.

'Katherine isn't going to be very happy that you were in late last night,' I said. 'It looks bad, Jess, if this early on you can't even stick to coming back at the agreed time. They're going to expect a lot more from you. As Jimmy gets older they're going to want to see you getting him into some sort of a bedtime routine. But you're sticking two fingers up at them and saying you'll do what you want. So tell me, what is it you actually want?'

'I want me, Darren and Jimmy to be together,' she said. 'To live together as a family.'

'Well, Social Services have got serious concerns about your parenting, so you've got to realise that until you start co-operating with them and show them that you're capable of looking after Jimmy, that is never going to happen,' I said.

I knew Jess thought I was being hard on her, but she needed to know the worst-case scenario.

'I love Darren so much, and it's so hard not being with him,' she sighed. 'I still don't see why me and Jimmy can't live with him at his place.'

'We've been through all this,' I said. 'Social Services have deemed it unsuitable for Jimmy.'

No matter how blunt I'd been with her, I knew I wasn't a patch on how Katherine was going to be.

'I'm very disappointed in you, Jess,' she told her when she arrived. 'It was only your second night at Maggie's and you were an hour late. You have to be in by 9 p.m. at the very latest tonight, and if you're not then Maggie will be reporting you missing to the police.'

'But that's not fair,' wailed Jess. 'When you made me go into care you said I only had to sleep here. You keep changing the rules.'

'I think 9 p.m. is late enough to be out with a four-day-old baby, especially when you've been at Darren's house most of the day,' she said. 'As Jimmy gets older, you'll need to be back by seven so that you can start getting him into a proper bedtime routine.'

'You can't tell me what to do – it's my baby,' said Jess, tears pricking her eyes. 'You can't make me come back here.'

'No, you're right, we can't make you,' Katherine told her. 'But hopefully you will understand that if you don't start working with us then we have to start questioning whether you're a fit parent for Jimmy.'

Jess burst into tears.

'You can't take my baby off me,' she sobbed, running out of the kitchen and storming upstairs.

My heart went out to her. She was a frightened little girl with no one to turn to, and it must have felt like the world was against her.

'It's beyond me why we're even having to go through all this,' sighed Katherine. 'We all know the way it's going to go in the end.'

It infuriated me that Katherine had assumed from the start that Jess was never going to be a good enough mum to Jimmy. I was so desperate to prove her wrong, but Jess wasn't doing herself any favours.

'Hopefully she's got the message and she'll be back on time tonight,' I said.

'If she isn't, then you need to report it,' said Katherine.

'What do you reckon?' I said. 'Shall I give her until eleven before I phone the police?'

'Nope,' said Katherine. 'Ten. Let's give her an hour's grace and no more. Jess needs to understand that it's serious and that her behaviour has repercussions.'

When Katherine had gone, Jess came downstairs.

'I'm going to Darren's now,' she said. 'Don't worry, I'll be back for 9 p.m. I promise.'

'Thank you,' I said. 'If you're having any problems getting back, then ring me.'

'Darren ain't got a phone,' she said. 'Anyway, I should be fine. I'll probably get a lift.'

I'd got out the car seat for her and attached it to the buggy frame.

'Have a good day, and see you tonight,' I told her.

All I could do was put my trust in her and hope that the message had got through.

That night it was like déjà vu when 9 p.m. came and went.

Please don't do this again, Jess, I thought.

Had nothing anyone said this morning sunk in? She was playing into Katherine's hands. By five past ten I knew I had no other choice but to pick up the phone. There was a certain procedure I had to follow to report a foster placement missing.

First of all I rang my agency's out-of-hours number. I spoke to one of the workers, who took all the details, and they would then call the Emergency Duty Team at Social Services. Afterwards I phoned the police and they put me through to my local station.

'I'd like to report a missing young person,' I said.

I explained that I was a foster carer and that Jess was a vulnerable sixteen-year-old with a newborn baby who had only been with me for two days.

'The night team are just coming on shift, but we'll send some officers round to have a chat to you when they're free,' she said.

I knew from experience that it could potentially take hours depending on what else was happening. A troubled teenager who hadn't come home probably wasn't high up on their list of priorities. I knew I was in for a long night, so all I could do was sit and wait. I was sure Jess was probably making a point and was still at Darren's house, but I had to do what Katherine had requested, and the main issue was that a newborn baby was out so late.

It was midnight before a couple of officers turned up.

'Can you describe Jess to me?' one of them asked.

'She's about five foot two with short blonde hair. She was wearing jeans and a T-shirt and hoodie. The baby's four days old and called Jimmy.'

'Have you got any idea about where she might be?' he asked.

'I suspect she's at her boyfriend Darren's house,' I said. 'She was due back at 9 p.m. and she and the baby aren't allowed to spend the night there.'

I gave them Darren's address, and Jess's mum's contact details just in case. Both had been given to me at the placement meeting.

'As I'm sure you know, I'm afraid we're going to have to search the house now,' said one of the officers.

'Look, I saw Jess walk out of the door this morning with the baby and she's been out all day,' I said. 'I can assure you she's definitely not here.'

'I'm afraid we have to follow procedure, just like you do,' he said.

Although I knew it was a complete waste of time in this case, whenever I reported a young person missing officers always had to do a thorough search of the house. It was a measure that had been brought in throughout the country after police had spent hours searching for young people and then it had turned out they were hiding under a bed or in a cupboard at home just to cause a bit of drama and upset.

I understood why they had to do it, but it drove me demented. In the past when I'd fostered persistent runaways I'd have police turning up and searching the house several times a week. If I thought there was any possibility Jess was in the house, I would have searched it myself before calling them and wasting their time.

It was also terrifying for other children who had lived with me over the years. Imagine waking up in the middle of the night and seeing two police officers standing in your bedroom? Louisa was still awake so I was able to explain to her what was happening, but Lily was fast asleep.

'We'll be as quiet as we can,' the officers assured me as they crept round her bedroom with torches.

I went in there with them just in case she woke up and was frightened, but thankfully she didn't stir. My new house was a lot bigger than my old place so it took them nearly an hour to search every room, including the loft, and look under beds and in every cupboard and wardrobe. Unsurprisingly there was no sign of Jess or Jimmy.

'We'll go round to the boyfriend's place first and let you know how we get on,' the officer told me.

Before they left they gave me an incident number which I then passed on to my agency and the local authority. It was proof that I'd called it in and had done what was expected of me.

By the time the police left it was after one and I was shattered. I wrapped myself up in a blanket and sat up watching TV in the front room.

An hour later my mobile rang and I pounced on it. It was the police.

'Have you found her?' I asked.

34

'Unfortunately Jess and the baby weren't at her boyfriend's house,' the officer told me.

'What do you mean?' I asked. 'Was Darren there?'

'There was no sign of any of them, and let's just say the other residents of the house weren't very helpful when it came to telling us where they might be.'

'Have you tried her mum's?' I asked.

'I'm afraid there was no answer at that address.'

The officer said they had another incident to attend to but that they'd go back later to Darren's house and try again.

'Maybe after a second wake-up call they'll feel like being more helpful and tell us where they are,' he said.

I prayed he was right. I was really worried now. I had assumed Jess was making a point by spending the night at Darren's, but she could be anywhere. All I could do was sit tight and hope that she and Jimmy were safe.

I must have nodded off because suddenly I woke up with a start on the sofa. My mobile was ringing next to my head. It was 4 a.m.

'It's the police,' said a voice. 'We're at your front door but there was no answer.'

He hung up before I could ask whether they'd got Jess and the baby. I ran to the front door and opened it. Much to my relief, there was a tired-looking Jess flanked by two police officers. One of them was carrying the car seat, in which Jimmy was fast asleep.

'Thank God,' I said. 'Where on earth have you been?'

'One of her boyfriend's brothers told us that they were at his mate's house so we picked them up there.'

'Oh, Jess,' I said. 'What on earth were you thinking? I've been so worried.'

She looked down at the floor and didn't say anything.

'We've had a word with the young lady about the importance of returning back here on a night, and pointed out that we're not a taxi service,' said one of the officers sternly.

'Thank you for all your help,' I told them before closing the door.

Jess stood in the hallway looking sheepish.

'What did you call them for?' she asked.

'I told you yesterday – I have to, it's my job,' I said. 'Katherine and I clearly told you what would happen if you were late, and worse than that, you didn't even bother coming back at all and thought you could get away with it.'

I was disappointed with her rather than angry, plus I was exhausted.

'I'm too tired to talk about this any more now,' I said. 'Let's go to bed and we'll chat in the morning. Is Jimmy OK?' I asked.

'He's fine,' she said. 'He's been asleep for hours. It was horrible being woken up by them police. I'm knackered.'

'That makes two of us,' I said. 'I'll go and settle Jimmy if you want to have a wash or get a quick drink.'

'Ta,' she said.

Really I wanted to make sure for myself that the baby was fine. Thankfully Jimmy seemed unscathed by the ordeal. He didn't stir as I lifted him out of the car seat and placed him in the Moses basket.

Before I went to bed, I had to text my agency to let them know Jess was back. They would then email Katherine so she'd know exactly what had happened when she arrived at the office in the morning.

As I walked back upstairs, Jess came out of the bathroom in her pyjamas.

'Night, Maggie,' she said. 'I'm really sorry.'

'Let's get some sleep and we'll talk about it tomorrow,' I told her.

As I closed my bedroom door, I suddenly realised that it was already tomorrow and Katherine was bound to be round in a few hours. When she got to work and saw the update about what had happened overnight, there was no doubt about it – she was going to be on the warpath.

FOUR

Learning to be Mummy

Three short hours of sleep later, I had to be up to see the girls off to school and college. Thankfully one of Lily's friends' mums was taking her today, and I'd just waved her and Louisa off when Jess stumbled out of her bedroom. She looked as shattered as I felt.

'How are you feeling?' I asked. 'I don't know about you, but I'm exhausted.'

'I'm really sorry that you're tired,' she said. 'I didn't know the police were gonna come and get me. I wanted to be with Darren, and I thought it would be OK if we weren't at his house.'

I wasn't angry with her, just increasingly frustrated. I had to keep reminding myself of what she'd been through in the past few days. She was a scared, vulnerable, sixteen-year-old girl who didn't have any family support or money. All she had in the world was her boyfriend, so it was understandable that she wanted to be with him. While most teenagers her age were worrying about GCSEs and whether they'd got the latest trainers, she was responsible for a newborn baby. She was like a frightened rabbit caught in the headlights, unsure which way to turn.

'Let's get some breakfast,' I said. 'I'll feel better after a strong cup of coffee.'

Jess was giving Jimmy a bottle and I was making her some toast when there was a sharp knock at the door. Jess and I looked at each other. We both knew exactly who that was going to be.

'I'll take Jimmy if you like,' I said.

He'd finished his bottle by now so I put him over my shoulder and went to answer the door.

As brusque and efficient as ever, Katherine marched into the kitchen.

'I got to work this morning to find an email from Maggie's agency about last night's antics with the police,' she told Jess. 'I can't begin to tell you how disappointed I am.

'You've only been at Maggie's three days, but you've hardly spent any time here. You can't be out late or out overnight with a newborn baby and no one knowing where you are. It's just not on. So, as you've given me no other choice, this is what we're going to do.'

She slammed a piece of paper down on the kitchen table.

'What is it?' asked Jess, looking terrified.

'It's a contract,' said Katherine. 'A contract between you and Social Services so that you know exactly what's expected of you.'

Contracts were often used with teenagers as a way to re-iterate what the rules were. It was an agreement between Social Services and the placement, and both Jess and Katherine had to sign it. Writing it down seemed to make things more official somehow, and it meant the rules were very clear and there were no ambiguities. Also, if Jess didn't abide by the contract or refused to sign it, it would be more evidence of her refusal to co-operate with the local authority.

'Have a read and then we'll talk it through,' she told her.

I had a quick glance at it over her shoulder.

Jimmy must attend all midwife and health visitor appointments.

Jimmy must be back in the placement by 7 p.m. every night.

Maggie to phone out-of-hours if Jimmy isn't back in the placement by 7 p.m.

Jess must agree not to leave the placement before 10 a.m.

Jess must establish a bath and bedtime routine for Jimmy as soon as possible.

The emphasis was mostly on Jimmy, so if Jess didn't stick to it, I knew it would be used as evidence that she wasn't putting Jimmy's needs ahead of her own.

Jess shook her head as she read it.

'I can't believe you're doing this,' she said. 'You're changing things every day. It's so unfair.'

'I'm afraid you forced us into it after what happened last night,' said Katherine. 'We told you from the start that you and Jimmy were not allowed to stay overnight at Darren's house.'

'But we wasn't at Darren's house. We were at his mate's.'

'And we know nothing about this so-called mate, or whether his house is a suitable place to take a newborn baby,' said Katherine. 'Our job is to protect you and Jimmy and make sure both of you are safe. Therefore it's important that we know where you are at all times. You were supposed to be back here last night, and you weren't.'

With that, Katherine got a pen out of her handbag and passed it to Jess.

'I've already signed it. Now it's your turn.'

Jess hesitated.

'I haven't really got much choice, have I?' she muttered.

She scrawled her name on the bottom, threw down the pen and stormed off upstairs.

'Let's hope the contract works,' said Katherine. 'Although I've got a feeling it's not going to make one iota of difference to Jess. She seems intent on doing what she wants, when she wants, regardless of the rules.'

'There was one thing I was wondering that I thought might help,' I said. 'Could Darren come round here?'

Katherine looked incredulous.

'Why on earth would you want him to do that?' she asked.

'It's just a suggestion, but I thought it might encourage Jess to spend more time here with Jimmy. If all three of them are here, then I can keep a closer eye on things. Jess has hardly been here, so I have no way of assessing her parenting,' I said.

'I would have to put restrictions on it, of course,' I added. 'If I said Darren could come over at 6 p.m. then he would have to be gone by eight. As long as he didn't prove to be a problem, then it might work. He could help Jess get Jimmy settled into a bedtime routine.'

'Let's see whether this contract works first,' said Katherine. 'Rather than encouraging them to play happy families, Jess needs to prove to us that she's responsible enough to stick to rules and get Jimmy and herself back here for the correct time. If she can't, then we'll seriously have to look at taking Jimmy into care. We can't risk anything happening to him.'

'OK,' I sighed, but I really hoped it wouldn't come to that.

I looked down at Jimmy, who was now fast asleep in my arms. Although I didn't like the way Katherine was handling this situation, there were elements of it that I agreed with. At the heart of all this was a tiny baby who needed protecting. As he got older, Jimmy would need routine and consistency and to go to sleep in the same room every night. No one would agree that it was good for a newborn to be on a bus late at night or woken up at two in the morning and put into a police car.

After Katherine had gone, I went upstairs to see Jess. She was always polite to me and she was never stroppy like she was towards Katherine. I knew that the contract had really upset her and I could see that she'd been crying. I put Jimmy down in the Moses basket and went and sat on the bed.

'Do you want to talk about it?' I asked.

'No,' she said, turning her face away from me so I couldn't see her tears.

'Jess, it's so important that you stick to this contract so you can prove to Katherine that you're a good mum who puts her baby's needs before her own,' I told her. 'Keeping your newborn son out until all hours isn't showing her that. Do you want to lose custody of Jimmy?'

'No,' she snapped. 'I'd die if they took my baby away. I love him so much.'

'Well then, you need to do what Social Services are asking you,' I said.

I suspected Jess would be leaving soon to go and see Darren.

'What time are you going to Darren's today?' I asked.

'I ain't,' she said sadly. 'He's gone away with his brothers to look at some cars and bikes they want to buy. They'll be gone all weekend.'

It was Friday now, so that gave me three whole days with Jess without her disappearing off. It would finally give me a chance to get to know her better and to see how she was around Jimmy. I'd only seen her first thing in the morning and last thing at night, and I didn't have a clue what happened to the baby in the day or how well he was being cared for. She'd hardly seen Lily and Louisa, as she'd been out of the house most of the time since she arrived.

'I've got an idea to cheer you up,' I said. 'How about we go into town and get a few bits for you and Jimmy? You could both do with a few more clothes.'

'There's no need to do that,' she said. 'You can't be spending your money on us.'

'It's fine,' I reassured her. 'Social Services give me a weekly allowance for you in case you need anything.'

I knew how little she and Jimmy had actually brought with them.

'The girls are at school now, and Lily's at a sleepover tonight so I don't have to rush back,' I said.

'Are you sure?' she asked.

'Sure I'm sure.' I smiled.

We drove into town. I pushed the buggy round Next while Jess chose some Babygros and little outfits for Jimmy. She picked out a teddy bear mobile for his room and I bought her a changing bag so she didn't have to carry bottles and nappies around in a carrier. Then I took her to H&M and encouraged her to pick out a few things for herself.

'This is really nice.' She smiled. 'I ain't never had new clothes, just stuff my mum or Darren's mum gave me when they didn't want them no more. But I'm worried you're spending too much on us. You won't have nothing left for the other kids.'

'I get a clothing allowance for each child I look after, so don't worry – you're not taking it away from anyone else,' I told her.

Jess was different to most teenagers that I'd fostered, who expected you to buy them everything new and were continually asking for things.

'If you end up staying with us for a while we could pay your allowance into your bank account and you could come shopping yourself,' I said.

'Would I be allowed to buy Daz some clothes too, as he doesn't have no money?' she asked.

'I'm afraid the allowance is just for you and Jimmy,' I said.

'Darren's mum gets money for him but he never sees none of it,' she told me. 'He helps his brothers do jobs and sometimes they give him money but he used all that to buy things for me and the baby.'

My heart went out to these two teenagers and the pressure they must have felt in the lead-up to Jimmy's birth. It was clear that they'd been left to cope alone.

During our shopping trip I also bought Jess a simple pay-as-you-go mobile phone.

'If you're going out to Darren's with Jimmy then I would feel a lot happier if I could text or ring you just to check where you are,' I said. 'Then you can ring me if the bus is late or you're having problems getting back. I'll give Katherine and the midwife your number, too, so they know they've always got a way of contacting you.'

Jess seemed delighted with the phone, although not the fact that Katherine would have her new number.

'I'm not sure what Daz is going to say when he sees all my new stuff,' she said.

'What do you mean?' I asked.

'He don't like charity, and he might not like you buying me and Jimmy things.'

'Well, why don't you explain to him that I have to buy you things you need, otherwise your social worker won't be very happy with me because that money I get is to help you.'

'I suppose when you put it like that he'll be OK.' She smiled.

Jess texted Darren to tell him about the shopping trip and to give him her new number. She grinned when a message beeped back.

'He said to say thank you for buying me and Jimmy all our new stuff, and it's OK with him as he doesn't want you to get a bollocking from the social worker,' she said.

'I've already told him what a bitch she is,' she added, and I couldn't help but smile.

We went home and Jess changed Jimmy's nappy and put him in the bouncy chair where he quickly nodded off. Jess seemed restless and didn't know what to do with herself.

'What shall I do now?' she asked.

'Do you fancy making some cakes?' I suggested.

'Cakes?' she said, laughing. 'I ain't made those since I was a little girl at school.'

'Come on,' I said. 'It will be fun.'

Jess helped me measure out the ingredients.

'Did you ever bake with your mum?' I asked as she mixed it all together.

'Nah,' she scoffed. 'She's not really the baking type. She was smacked off of her head most of the time so I brought myself up, really.'

Just as she was spooning the mixture into the bun cases, Jimmy stirred and began to cry. I didn't say anything and waited to see how Jess would respond. She ignored him and carried on with the cakes. Eventually when the crying got even louder, Jess looked over at him.

'No, Jimmy,' she snapped. 'You'll have to wait. I'm busy.'

I was a bit taken aback and shocked by the harsh tone of voice that she'd spoken to him in.

'When did Jimmy last have a bottle?' I asked her.

'When we was in town,' she said.

'That was four hours ago, so do you think he might be crying because he's hungry?'

'Maybe,' said Jess. 'But Darren's mum said not to pick babies up when they're crying or they'll get used to it and then they'll be spoilt little brats.'

'Jess, where was Jimmy a week ago?' I asked.

She looked at me, puzzled by my question.

'Inside my tummy,' she said.

'And now he's in the big wide world and he's probably crying because he wants his mummy and some warm milk and that's what he's trying to tell you.'

'Oh,' she said. 'I didn't think.'

Jess quickly put the spoon down and went over to Jimmy. As soon as she picked him up, the crying stopped. She looked over at me.

'You was right,' she said. 'He wanted a cuddle.'

I warmed up a bottle and as Jess fed him, I talked to her about why babies cry.

'Little babies Jimmy's age cry because they want something. That might be a cuddle with their parent, they might be tired or have wind or be hungry or want a nappy change,' I told her.

'But how do I know what he wants?' she asked. 'It all sounds the same to me.'

'After a while you'll get to know what he's crying for,' I explained. 'And if you don't, you can rule things out, like remembering the last time he had a bottle or checking his nappy or noticing if he's yawning or rubbing his eyes like he needs a sleep.

'Most of all at this age he just wants to be near you, so whatever else, if he's crying like that pick him up and give him a cuddle. Newborns get a lot of comfort from being close to their mummies and hearing their heartbeat, like they did when they were in the womb.'

I'd had several mother-and-baby placements over the years, and it was like a crash course in parenting. In a way, the easy part was teaching them all the practical things, like how to change a nappy and making up and sterilising bottles. It was the emotional side of things that was harder. Having Jess there over the weekend enabled me to see where she needed help.

When I went into her room on Saturday morning with some clean washing I noticed there was a pile of rolled-up dirty nappies on the floor.

'Please could you put those in the bin?' I asked. 'It's not hygienic having them all over the floor and they're starting to smell.'

'OK,' she said. 'Sorry.'

The one thing I quickly noticed about Jess was that she was always happy to do things when I reminded her and she didn't complain. When I looked in the Moses basket, the fitted sheet was covered in sick.

'Here's a clean sheet for Jimmy,' I said. 'It's really important to change them regularly – I change our bedding once a week.'

'Really?' gasped Jess in shock – I think she thought I was being over the top.

'How often does Darren change his sheets?' I asked.

Jess shrugged.

'Dunno,' she said. 'I've never seen him do it. Maybe he takes them to the launderette when I'm not there.'

She also needed a bit of guidance around bottles. When I looked in the carrier bag that she'd taken to Darren's a few days ago, it was filled with dirty bottles with curdled milk in the bottom.

'Do you mind washing these bottles and then putting them in the steriliser?' I asked her.

I watched her give them a quick swill under the cold tap and then plonk them in the sterilising unit.

'Jess, you need to give them a proper wash and rinse with hot water before you put them in,' I said.

I showed her how to use a brush and get into all the nooks and crannies.

'Otherwise the powder will get caught in the rim and the teat and it will give Jimmy tummy ache,' I explained.

Louisa, who was watching all this with interest, rolled her eyes.

'Argh, don't you even know how to do that?' she said. 'Next you'll be saying you don't know how to change a nappy.'

'Louisa, don't be mean,' I told her. 'Jess is doing a great job.'

Jess looked close to tears.

'Don't let her upset you,' I told her when Louisa had left the room. 'Ever since she's been doing her childcare course she thinks she's an expert on babies and children.'

'I'm trying to do it right, Maggie,' she told me. 'Honestly I am. But it's really hard. There's so much stuff to remember.'

'I know you are, love,' I said. 'No one expects you to be perfect. I'm not judging you, remember – I'm on your side.'

She kept forgetting to change the water in the sterilising unit and put the fluid in, so I put up a sticker chart on the wall and told her to put a gold star on it each day when she'd changed it.

'I'm not treating you like a toddler,' I told her. 'But it's a way of me knowing if you've done it or not because I can't check with you if you're out.'

I could tell she was desperate to do everything properly and to prove to me that she was a good mum.

Like I said, the practical side of things was the easy part. The hardest part was teaching mums how to interact with their babies. Most of the young women I worked with hadn't had good childhoods. Jess had been in and out of care all her life and didn't have any kind of model to base her parenting on. She didn't understand the importance of interacting with Jimmy. Even little Lily did it instinctively. When Jimmy was sitting in his bouncy chair in the living room, she stopped to talk to him and tickle his toes. Whereas Jess was very quiet around him and didn't chitter-chatter away naturally to him.

That Saturday afternoon I watched Jess change Jimmy's nappy.

'When you're cleaning his bum it's a good time for you to have a little chat with him,' I said.

Jess looked at me like I was mad.

'Why would I do that?' she said. 'He's a baby. He can't talk. Anyway, what would I say to him?'

'It's less about what you say and more about him hearing your voice and watching your mouth and the sounds you make.

Look, watch this,' I said, going over to Jimmy and sticking my tongue out.

His little eyes watched me intently and after I'd done it a few times, he stuck his own tongue out to copy me. Jess was amazed.

'You see,' I said. 'Even tiny babies thrive on communication.'

With teenage mums like Jess it was often more effective to teach by example, so I offered to take over the nappy changing.

'If you don't know what to say, you could just chat to him about what you're doing,' I suggested.

'Hello, Jimmy. How are you today?' I said. 'Shall we change your nappy? Have you got a wet bottom? Oh, poor Jimmy, let's get you all nice and clean.'

Jess rolled her eyes at me. I was being deliberately over the top to get my point across, but I hoped that she'd got the idea.

'Babies love singing too,' I told her.

'No way,' said Jess. 'I ain't singing to him. I'd feel stupid.'

I hoped that in time it would come. I knew none of this was because she didn't care.

I got a few things out of the loft for Jimmy like a play mat, some toys to dangle from the handle of his car seat and a fabric black and white book.

'What's the point in reading to him?' she scoffed. 'It's a waste of time.'

'Tiny babies love looking at black and white,' I said. 'He's only little now, but as he gets older he'll love all these toys and they'll help his development.'

I could see she was taking it all on board.

Sometimes she was a typical teenager and just didn't think. On Sunday night she washed her hair and came downstairs to blow-dry it. I'd been upstairs on the second floor sorting out some washing but as I came downstairs I heard Jimmy crying. It wasn't just normal newborn cries, though, it was hysterical wailing.

I rushed into the living room. Jess was sat on the settee with the hairdryer on. She had her back to Jimmy, who was lying behind her on the sofa. He was screaming his head off. His face was bright red, his fists were clenched and he was kicking his little legs. I turned off the hairdryer at the plug.

Jess jumped when she heard Jimmy's screams.

'Jess, he's absolutely hysterical here,' I said. 'He's probably terrified by the noise of the hairdryer, and look where he's lying.'

The sofa cushion was on a slant where Jess was sitting on it and Jimmy had rolled back towards the gap between the cushion and the frame.

'He could have fallen down the gap at the back of the settee and been smothered by the cushions,' I told her. 'He'd have been much safer in the Moses basket.'

'I didn't do it on purpose,' she said. 'I didn't hear him crying, honest. I wasn't ignoring him.'

She was beside herself.

'Jess, it's OK,' I said. 'I just want you to think carefully about things before you do them. No one expects you to be the perfect mum. Do you think older mums in their twenties and thirties know what to do? They're learning too, and we all make mistakes. I'm afraid you've got me here to point yours out.'

Jess smiled.

'I just want to show you that I can do it,' she said. 'That I love Jimmy and that I can be responsible.'

'I can tell you love Jimmy,' I said. 'I can see that by how upset you are at the thought that you might have hurt him.'

She was trying her very best. But unfortunately I felt that Katherine wasn't prepared to see that, and that maybe Jess's best was just not going to be good enough in the end.

FIVE

A Visit from Daddy

As a foster carer, I can teach a mother how to look after her baby, how to perform all the tasks correctly like bottle washing, bathing and nappy changing, but the one thing you can't teach is love. That all-consuming, primordial desire to protect your baby no matter what has to come from deep inside the mum herself, and no one can teach her that.

After spending a few days with Jess, the one thing I was sure about was that she loved her baby. I could see it in little things, like the way she looked at Jimmy when he was in her arms having a bottle, how she hovered around him nervously when someone else like Louisa or Katherine was holding him. I could see it in the way she stroked his cheek when she said goodnight to him or noticed that the sun was shining in his eyes when he was sitting in his bouncer in the kitchen one day. They were just tiny little things, but they all showed me that she was attached to her baby. She might not be able to make the perfect bottle and sometimes she made silly decisions, but the bottom line was that I could see she loved Jimmy fiercely. So that's why, after that first weekend, I became determined to help her fight her corner with Social Services. The rest would come.

I just hoped that I'd made her see sense, and that she now knew how important it was for her to obey the contract and show Katherine that she was willing to co-operate. I'd enjoyed spending the weekend with her. However, once Darren was back, the real test was to come. I could tell Jess was itching to see him after being apart for three days. She couldn't wait to get round there on Monday morning.

'I've missed him so much,' she said.

'I know you have,' I said. 'Have a lovely day together, but please remember to be back here by seven.'

'Maggie, I will,' she told me. 'I promise I won't let you down.'

I was on tenterhooks all day worrying about whether she would be back on time, and all the repercussions there would be if I had to phone it in again and call the police. I was so relieved when she came in right on the dot of seven as well as feeling a bit guilty for ever doubting her.

Thankfully Jess came back on time every night that week, and it enabled us to get Jimmy into a good bedtime routine. He was fed, bathed and in his cot by 7.30 p.m.

'You've done so well,' I told Jess on Friday night. 'I know how hard it is for you to leave Darren's. Why don't you see if he'd like to come back with you one night next week for a couple of hours?'

'What?' she said, looking shocked. 'Come back here, to this house? Would that really be allowed?'

'I don't see why not,' I said. 'He could come back with you at 6 p.m., stay for tea then help you give Jimmy a bath and put him to bed.'

'I don't believe it,' she said, looking really chuffed. 'That would be ace.'

'Well, you've been sticking to the rules and showing us that you can be responsible, so I can be a little bit flexible every now and again.'

'But what about Katherine?' asked Jess. 'Will it be OK with her? I bet she won't allow it.'

'Don't worry, I'll clear it with Katherine,' I said.

I had a plan up my sleeve. At the weekend I phoned Becky at the agency. I wanted to discuss my concerns about Katherine with her and flag it up that I wasn't happy about the way she was handling the case.

'I don't feel like she's giving Jess a fair go,' I told her. 'She's so harsh with her, and she causes so much upset and confrontation when she comes round.

'Then in response to that, Jess is really bolshie and challenges her, which is not how she is when she's with me. So it means that Katherine never sees the positive side of Jess. But I can't help thinking, does she actually want to, or is her mind already made up?'

I still felt like Jess was fighting a losing battle.

'I believe Katherine's come to this placement with preconceived ideas that, no matter what Jess does, they're going to go for adoption for Jimmy.'

'What do you think?' asked Becky. 'I know it's early days, but what's your gut instinct?'

'She's a good little mum and she loves her baby,' I said. 'When she cocks up it's because she doesn't know, not because she doesn't care, and as you and I know, there's a heck of a lot of difference.

'Also when I teach her things about the baby and how to look after him, that information goes in and she gets it. Jimmy is happy and healthy, but Katherine isn't listening to any of this – she's just focusing on the negative.'

I explained that, after a rocky start, Jess had been trying really hard to stick to the terms of the contract and had come in on time every night this week.

'I think it would be really good for her if Darren could come round one evening to my house and help her with the bedtime routine,' I said. 'That would also give me an opportunity to meet him and see them together.

'She's got her act together and done what was expected of her, so it would be nice to be able to offer her some reward, and hopefully that would be an incentive to keep to the contract in future.'

'It sounds fair enough to me,' said Becky. 'Leave it with me and I'll have a chat to Katherine.'

One of the benefits of working for a fostering agency was having someone like Becky who could liaise with Social Services on my behalf. Having a buffer between us was really useful when I had a tricky social worker like Katherine to deal with.

Later on that day Becky called me back.

'OK, Katherine is fine with Darren coming round for tea one night next week and helping with Jimmy's bedtime,' she told me. 'If it goes well then she said we could perhaps look at making it a regular arrangement.'

'Wow,' I gasped. 'How did you manage that?'

'Let's just say we had a very long and involved discussion and in the end Katherine saw sense,' she told me.

'I can't wait to tell Jess,' I said.

Jess was as surprised as me when I told her the news.

'I'm gonna text Daz right now to tell him,' she said.

'When you speak to him, will you ask him what he does or doesn't like to eat?' I said.

'Oh, don't worry, he'll eat anything.' She smiled.

It was lovely to see Jess so happy, and I think that was the first time I'd seen her smile since she'd arrived. We arranged for Darren to come round the following Monday and I decided to cook spaghetti Bolognese for tea.

I knew Darren's impending visit had given Jess a boost, and she made sure she was back both nights over the weekend as she was determined nothing was going to jeopardise it.

Before they left for school and college on Monday morning, I told Lily and Louisa about the visit.

'Jess's boyfriend Darren is coming round for tea tonight, so we all need to be nice and welcoming to him,' I said.

Louisa rolled her eyes.

'I hope they won't be all over each other in front of us,' she groaned.

'They had better not be,' I said.

'Will he play Kerplunk with me?' asked Lily.

'Maybe,' I laughed. 'You'll have to ask him when he comes.'

The doorbell rang at 6 p.m. on the dot. Jess was stood there with the buggy, hand in hand with Darren, and they both looked very nervous. Darren was tall, blond and lanky with bad acne. He looked so young, standing there in his baseball hat, jeans and T-shirt.

'You must be Darren,' I said. 'I'm Maggie. Come in, it's lovely to meet you.'

He looked very shy and awkward, standing there shuffling his feet, and he wouldn't make eye contact with me.

'Go on,' said Jess, forcing him through the front door. 'Go in.'

'You've got a beautiful son,' I told him.

'Oh, er, thanks,' he said.

As he walked past me I was hit by the overpowering smell of body spray and I thought it was very sweet that he'd made such an effort.

They went through to the living room while I made them a cup of tea.

When I came back in, Darren was sitting on the sofa with Jess. He had his arm around her and he was holding Jimmy on his lap.

'How was your day?' I asked him.

''S all right,' he said.

'What have you and Jess been up to?'

'Not much really,' he sighed. 'Just chillin'.'

He was very polite but he was a typical monosyllabic teenager. I couldn't work out whether he was shy or nervous, but he certainly wasn't the cocky, arrogant young lad that I'd been expecting.

As the night went on, thankfully Darren seemed to relax a little bit. It was nice to see that he was happy holding Jimmy and he made sure he carefully supported his head. I was impressed with the way he handed the baby to Jess when I gave him his cup of tea.

'I don't want to drop none on my boy,' he said.

I didn't want to ruin the mood, but there were a few things that I needed to let him and Jess know.

'I'm so pleased that you were able to come round,' I said. 'But as this is a fostering house and there are other children here, there's a couple of things I need to mention.

'If you go upstairs with Jess, I expect the bedroom door to remain open at all times, and just to let you know that I will probably be hovering around too.

'It's not that I don't trust you,' I told him. 'It's just that I've got other children in the placement as well and you haven't been vetted by Social Services. Is that OK?'

It was also because I didn't think it was appropriate for a young lad to be in a teenage girl's bedroom under my roof.

Darren looked surprised but he nodded.

'Thank you,' I said. 'And if any of that doesn't happen, then I'm afraid you won't be able to come here again. There are certain rules that I have to follow, and I'll be in trouble if I don't.'

While Jess and Darren chatted to the girls, I went into the kitchen to put the pasta on.

'Will one of you set the table for me?' I called.

'I'll do it,' yelled Jess.

'Well, what do you think?' she asked as she came into the kitchen. 'Do you like him?'

'He seems like a nice lad, and he's very hands-on with Jimmy, which is good,' I replied.

'Oh, Daz is great with babies,' she beamed. 'He's got loads of cousins, and one of his brothers has got kids so he's used to being around little ones.'

Soon we all sat down for dinner at the kitchen table. Darren hungrily tucked into his spag bol and cleared his plate at lightning speed.

'Gosh, you were ready for that.' I smiled.

'Sorry,' he said, blushing when he realised the rest of us had only had a few mouthfuls.

'Would you like seconds?' I asked.

'Yes please,' he said. 'I ain't eaten much today except some Monster Munch and a Mars Bar. My mum don't really cook, so I just get stuff from the shop if I've got any money.'

I got the impression food was scarce at his house, and I made a mental note to send Jess off with a packed lunch when she went round there.

After we'd cleared away the dinner things, I set the baby bath up on the kitchen table. It meant that Darren didn't need to be upstairs, and I could observe them giving Jimmy a bath without us all being crammed into the bathroom and them feeling like I was looking over their shoulder all the time.

I laid the changing mat and towel down at one end and Jess filled the bath with warm water. I'd already talked her through a bath time routine, and she'd been doing it for the past week. What was lovely to see was her explaining it all to Darren.

'Where's the wipes?' he asked as he took off Jimmy's nappy.

'No, Daz, we can't use wipes no more,' she told him. 'Maggie said they're too harsh for a little baby's skin so it's best to use cotton wool and water instead.'

'Oh, OK,' he said.

I smiled at the fact she'd remembered everything I'd told her and was now repeating it word for word to Darren. She showed him how to use cotton wool to clean Jimmy's eyes, behind his ears, under his nose and in the creases under his neck.

'That's where the milk dribbles and if you don't clean it, it goes all dry and crusty and makes their skin sore.'

'You're a right know-it-all these days, aren't you?' he teased, and I could see Jess was proud that she knew what she was doing.

I watched as Darren carefully lowered Jimmy into the water.

'Make sure you support his head, Daz,' Jess told him.

He might only have been a young lad, but he seemed to want to be involved in his son's life. As I watched them bath Jimmy together, I was struck by what a good team they made.

After Darren had finished drying him, Jess turned to me.

'Shall I give him a massage tonight, Maggie?' she asked.

'If you want, lovely,' I said.

She got out the olive oil and Darren laughed.

'Are you gonna cook him?' he joked.

'Maggie says it's really good for his dry skin,' she told him. 'You should see him, Daz, he really likes it. He looks all chilled out.'

I think Darren thought I was completely mad, but Jess showed him how to do a massage and, give him his due, he gave it a go. Afterwards Darren gave Jimmy a bottle downstairs and then they went to settle him in his cot. I followed them upstairs as I'd already warned them I would have to do, and sorted some washing on the landing while they were in Jimmy's bedroom. Jimmy was tired out by his bath and he went down straight away.

Afterwards we all sat in the living room.

'Have you got the baby monitor?' Louisa asked.

'Oh no,' said Jess, jumping up. 'I left it in the kitchen.'

'And make sure it's turned on,' she said smugly.

I shot Louisa a warning look to let her know that her input wasn't helpful and that she should stop interfering and give Jess a chance.

'Do you want a game of Kerplunk?' Lily asked Darren shyly.

'All right,' he said. 'But I'll probably beat you.'

When I glanced at my watch, I saw it was eight o'clock already. Darren and Lily were engrossed in Kerplunk and Jess and Louisa were watching them. I didn't want to be a spoilsport but I knew it was important that I stuck to the rules, just as Jess had to. When that particular game was over, I gave him a gentle reminder.

'Darren, it's ten past eight now so you need to be making a move,' I said.

'Oh,' he said. 'OK.'

Jess turned to me.

'Please, Maggie, can't he stay a bit longer?' she begged.

'Don't push it, Jess,' I said. 'I've got to stick to the rules. I don't want Darren's first visit here to be his last. Besides, you'll see him tomorrow when you go round to his place.'

'All right,' she sighed.

'It's been lovely to meet you,' I told Darren. 'I'll have a chat to Jess's social worker, but hopefully you can come round again soon.'

It genuinely had been nice to meet him and to see him, Jess and the baby together. Although they were practically kids themselves, I could sense the love and warmth there was between them. I could see they were each other's support in the chaotic lives of each of their families. It made me even more convinced that despite their age, Katherine needed to understand that they were committed to each other and wanted to be together.

'Could Darren come round every night?' Jess asked when he'd gone.

'Not every night, I'm afraid,' I said. 'But two or three times a week is fine by me, as long as I clear it with Katherine first. If things go well, then maybe one weekend he could come round for an afternoon too.'

I thought Jess would be really pleased with that idea, so I was puzzled when she burst into tears.

'Hey, what's wrong?' I asked gently. 'What is it?'

'It's not fair,' she snivelled. 'I want to be with Darren and Jimmy all the time like a normal, proper family.'

'Hopefully one day you will be,' I said. 'But for now you've got to convince Social Services that you're both responsible enough.'

'Sometimes I think it would be easier just to take Jimmy and walk out of here,' she said.

'Jess, you know that's not a good idea,' I told her. 'Where would you go? You don't have any money or a safe place to live. Social Services would definitely take Jimmy into care then.

'I'm afraid you need to sit this out, prove to them that you're committed to each other and the baby and hopefully they will eventually help the three of you get somewhere to live. Or they could possibly find you a place at a special unit where you can be together as a family.'

'They have places like that?' she asked.

'Yes, they're called family assessment centres,' I told her. 'But they won't even consider that option if they don't think you're committed.'

'I know Katherine thinks Darren's a bad 'un because of his family, but he's not like his brothers,' she said. 'He's looked after me more than my own mum ever did, and he'd never hurt me or Jimmy.'

'What was your mum like when you were growing up?' I asked her gently.

It was always important to try and find out as much about a child's background as they were prepared to tell you, as that would often influence how they were as a parent.

'She was never there,' she said. 'And if she was she'd be too out of it to do anything or she was busy entertaining her "boyfriends".'

Jess's eyes filled with tears as she remembered the past.

'She'd send me to my room because she said her boyfriend was coming round, but I couldn't understand why it was a different man every time. I remember coming out of my room one day to try and find something to eat and one of them cornered me in the kitchen. He was a horrible sweaty man with a big beer belly and he pressed himself right up against me. I could feel his smelly breath on my face and I was terrified.'

'You poor, poor girl,' I said. 'Did you tell your mum about it?'

'She was there too,' said Jess. 'She laughed and said that maybe one day when I was a bit older he should come round and see me as well as her. I was only eleven.'

'Jess, did any of these men ever hurt you?' I asked her gently.

If she had been abused, then I had a duty to pass that information on to Social Services.

'No,' she said. 'I soon learnt that a swift kick in the goolies was the best way to put them off.'

'What did your mum say when you told her that you were pregnant?' I asked.

'She told me to get rid of it,' said Jess. 'She said babies were a millstone around your neck, just like I'd been all these years. When I wouldn't have an abortion, she threw me out and said she never wanted to hear from me again.'

What kind of a mother throws their pregnant teenage daughter out onto the streets? But Jess's mum hardly sounded like a contender for 'mother of the year'. I found it was often the case that girls who'd had rough childhoods got pregnant at a young age. It was a deep yearning in them to have something or someone of their own to love and to love them back. Perhaps it replaced the pain of not having had a loving family themselves.

'So you see, all I've got is Darren,' said Jess. 'Him and Jimmy are my life now, and I want to be the best mum I can be.'

I longed to put my arms around her and tell her that everything was going to be all right. But I couldn't, because I didn't know that it was.

*

The next morning when Jess had gone to Darren's, Becky called for an update.

'So how did Darren's visit go?'

'It went well,' I said. 'He's a nice lad, and he genuinely seems to care about Jess and Jimmy. It seems to be a really positive relationship and I think he's good for her. He gives her a sense of belonging and builds her self-esteem up. He's the only one not questioning or doubting her mothering skills, and she has a sense of being a proper mummy when she's with him.'

'Great,' said Becky. 'I shall be passing all that information on to Katherine and singing his praises.'

'I'd really like Darren coming round to be a regular thing,' I said. 'Twice a week would be ideal, and perhaps one weekend visit.'

'I'll ask and see what she says,' Becky told me.

To my surprise, Katherine agreed, and Darren's visits became part of our routine. We were three weeks into it when one night I got a text from Jess. She and Darren were due to come back at 6 p.m. for dinner but she texted me at five.

Having tea at Daz's. C u later.

I sent a message back.

OK. See you at seven.

I wanted to make it clear as that was Jimmy's bedtime and the time specified on the contract that they had to be back. But 7 p.m. came and went and there was no sign of them. I tried ringing her but it went straight to voicemail.

'Jess, it's Maggie. I was wondering where you were as we'd agreed that you'd be back by seven. Give me a call if you're having problems.'

Don't do this, Jess, I told myself. *Don't mess this up now.*

I was disappointed in her, as she'd been doing so well recently. By 8 p.m. I knew I had no choice but to call it in to my agency. Even though I'd been in mobile contact with Jess, I still was obliged to report it.

'Give it until nine and if she's not back by then, call the police,' the duty worker told me.

At 8.15 p.m. my mobile beeped.

Soz on Xbox and lost track of time. On way back.

Half an hour later there was a faint knock at the door. A sheepish-looking Jess and Darren were standing there with Jimmy fast asleep in the car seat.

As Darren started to walk through the door, I stopped him.

'Er, where do you think you're going?' I said to him. 'It's too late for you to come in tonight, Darren. The idea was that you come round to help with Jimmy's bedtime, but it's way past that. You need to leave now so we can go and get your son to bed.'

'OK,' he said. 'Sorry, Maggie.'

'Goodnight, Darren,' I said.

As soon as I closed the door, the excuses started.

'We didn't see the time,' said Jess. 'And then . . .'

'Jess,' I interrupted, 'you can give me all the excuses under the sun but it doesn't matter. The deal is if you don't have tea here then you're back with Jimmy at 7 p.m. for his bedtime. You didn't stick to that.

'At the end of the day it's irrelevant why. I've had to report it to my agency that you're late, and that's going to be passed on to Katherine, and what's she going to say?

'Everything you've done over the past few weeks – being on time, Darren coming round here – has just been thrown away

66

because you've not kept to your side of the bargain. You've got to realise that your actions have consequences.'

'I do,' she sobbed.

'Well, it's too late,' I said.

Pushing the boundaries was typical teenage behaviour. However, Jess had to realise that this was going to have dangerous repercussions for her and Darren. Perhaps I'd put too much faith in them after all.

SIX

Meetings and Meltdowns

Katherine called the following morning when Jess had already left for Darren's house.

'I hear they were late back again,' she sighed. 'I don't know about you, Maggie, but I'm getting really tired of all this.'

'It's such a shame, as she's been doing so well,' I said. 'Darren didn't drop Jess back until 8.45 p.m. so I wouldn't let him come in.'

'Dropped?' asked Katherine. 'What do you mean?'

'Dropped, as in he always gives her a lift back to my place on a night,' I told her.

'What, in a car?' asked Katherine.

'Yes,' I said.

'Was he driving, or was there anyone else with them?'

'I didn't actually see them pull up last night but in the past when I have, it's just been the two of them and Jimmy in the car.

'Why?' I asked, puzzled by all the strange questions.

'I know for a fact that Darren hasn't got a driving licence and therefore he won't have tax or insurance,' sighed Katherine.

'He shouldn't even be on the roads, and God knows where he's even got the car from. I can well imagine.'

'Maybe he's passed his test recently,' I suggested, desperately hoping it was a misunderstanding.

'Maggie, he was cautioned by the police three months ago for driving without a licence or insurance, so I very much doubt it.

'They're not going to take kindly to the fact that he's doing it again and this time with a newborn baby in the back.'

It didn't look good. It was yet more ammunition for Katherine to build a case against them.

'What are you going to do?' I asked.

'I'm going to go and talk to Darren and then I'm going to have to pass this information on to the police,' she said.

I was furious with Darren and Jess for being so stupid and putting both themselves and Jimmy at risk. When Jess came back that night, I was ready to have it out with her.

'Did Katherine come round?' I asked.

'Dunno,' she said. 'We was out all day. Why?'

'She's on the warpath, and rightly so,' I said. 'I told her how Darren drives you home every night and she informed me that he doesn't have a driving licence or insurance and he's got into trouble about it in the past.'

I could tell by Jess's face that she knew she'd been rumbled.

'How could you be so stupid?' I said, my voice rising as I struggled to keep my anger and frustration in check. 'You shouldn't have got in the car with him.'

'He's fine,' she said. 'He's been driving for years.'

'Yes, but not legally,' I told her. 'Jess, the point is what he's doing is illegal and highly dangerous. Imagine if you were in an accident and something happened to you and Jimmy or another person?

He shouldn't be on the roads, and you should never have got into a car with him. Where did he even get the car from anyway?'

'Oh, he gets them from all over,' she said. 'I don't ask no questions. I'm just glad me and Jimmy don't have to catch the bus in the dark.'

I was furious with her for being so naive.

'Yes, Jess, but can't you see that by giving you a lift when he doesn't have a licence is a big risk?'

'That's just Daz,' she said. 'He don't mean no harm.'

I felt like I was banging my head against a brick wall. This rough diamond act wasn't going to cut it with Katherine.

'Katherine's coming round to speak to you first thing in the morning,' I said. 'So make sure you're here. And if I ever see you in a car with Darren driving then I will report it to Social Services straight away.'

When Katherine arrived the following day, she didn't waste any time beating about the bush.

'I'm not happy about what's been happening with the car, so I'm adding several more clauses into your contract. You and Jimmy are not to get in any car driven by Darren. Neither of you are to be dropped back here on an evening by Darren.

'From now on, you will both travel to and from Darren's house on the bus, and we'll sort you out a bus pass to cover the fare. Is that clear?'

'Yes,' said Jess meekly.

'As Darren's been breaking the law I have a duty to pass that information on to the police.'

Jess started to cry.

'You can't grass him up,' she sobbed. 'That's not fair, he might go to prison. Please don't tell the coppers.'

'Jess, I have to,' said Katherine. 'I'm going to go round now and explain all this to Darren.'

When Katherine left, Jess was beside herself with worry.

'I need to see Darren to check he's OK,' she said. 'What if he's been arrested already?'

I gave her some money for her bus fare and reminded her to be back at seven at the latest.

'If Darren's not at home then give me a ring or text me and I'll come and get you and Jimmy,' I said.

However, I didn't hear from Jess all day, and that evening I waited by the window. Part of me was still worried that they were going to turn up in a car and I wanted to double-check. I breathed a sigh of relief when I saw them walking down the road.

'What happened with the police?' I asked Darren.

'They came round and gave me a talking-to but they couldn't prove nothing as they didn't see me behind the wheel,' he told me. 'They said next time I won't be so lucky.'

'Well, I hope you're going to listen to them,' I said. 'This isn't going to do you any favours at all with Social Services.'

Katherine called me a few days later.

'Just to let you know we'll be holding the six-week review meeting next week,' she said. 'With all this car business and the constant lateness, I think we need to have a chat about the way things are going.'

The meeting couldn't have fallen at a worse time because of the lateness and the allegations that Darren had been driving illegally. It was being held at Social Services with myself, Katherine, Becky, Jess and Darren as well as an Independent Reviewing Officer – otherwise known as an IRO. The IRO is normally someone who works for Social Services but who hasn't been involved in the case so far. Every 'looked-after' child has to have a named IRO who keeps an eye on how the local authority manages their case, and also makes sure the child's views are taken into account. So far we hadn't met Jess's IRO, who was a woman called Kimberly.

A few days before the review meeting she came round to see Jess.

'What's she coming to see me for?' asked Jess. 'I don't want another person telling me off.'

'She's here for you, Jess,' I told her. 'She's come round to hear your views, so tell her if you've got any worries or concerns.'

Kimberly was in her fifties with grey hair and had a gentle, kind manner about her which I think helped put Jess at ease. They were chatting for over an hour in the living room.

'See you both at the meeting,' she said as she left.

'How did it go?' I asked Jess when she'd gone.

'She was dead nice,' she said. 'She asked me how it was going living here, and what I liked about it and what I wanted to happen. And she asked me what I thought about Katherine.'

'What did you say?' I asked.

'I told her the truth. I didn't call her a bitch or nothing but I said I thought she had it in for me and Daz from the start and she wanted to take Jimmy away from us, but that I just wanted us all to live together in our own place or at one of those special centres.'

I didn't mention my concerns to Kimberly about Katherine as I knew in reality that there was nothing she could really do about her. There was nothing anybody could do, because in theory Katherine wasn't doing anything wrong. In fact, on paper she was doing everything by the book. It was her general attitude and her constant ability to rile Jess and Darren that was the problem.

As carers, we're always taught when we're writing our recordings that it's got to be fact and not opinions. However, I felt Katherine was basing all her decisions on opinion and not fact, although that was very hard for me to prove.

In the days leading up to the meeting, I could see Jess was getting more and more nervous.

'What's it about?' she asked. 'What's she going to say? Are they going to take Jimmy away?'

'They can't just take your baby away,' I reassured her. 'It's a meeting with everyone involved in your case to talk about how things are going and how best to move forward. We always have one after a child has been in the placement for six weeks.'

To be honest, I was secretly worried about where all this was leading. I knew Katherine wasn't going to be complimentary about Jess's behaviour over the past six weeks. On the day of the meeting, Jess looked terrified. She and Darren sat there holding hands while Katherine welcomed everyone into the room. Jimmy was fast asleep in his buggy in the corner of the office.

'Jimmy is six weeks old now, and to be honest I don't feel as if we're any further forward,' said Katherine. 'Maggie is telling me that Jess has a strong bond with the baby and her parenting is good, but I've yet to see this for myself.

'Frankly all I'm seeing at the minute is a failure to turn up on time, a failure to stick to the rules and put Jimmy's needs before her own. That's not to mention putting his life at risk by getting into a car that's being driven illegally.'

'That's not fair,' muttered Darren. 'That was my fault.'

'Ssshh, Daz,' whispered Jess, squeezing his hand.

'So what I'd like them both to do is attend a family centre with Jimmy three times a week to start off with, from 9 a.m. until midday, where myself and other support workers can observe their parenting skills and address our concerns.'

'Shall we say that we'll have another meeting in six weeks to see how things are progressing?' suggested Kimberly, the IRO.

'That sounds reasonable,' said Katherine.

Darren shook his head and banged his fist down on the meeting table.

'You can't do this,' he shouted, jumping up off his chair. 'Jess has done everything that you asked, and I have as well. What more do you want us to do? Jump through even more hoops? Well I ain't f***ing having it.'

'You see what I mean,' Katherine said smugly to the IRO. 'If he can't control his temper in a meeting, what must he be like around a young baby?'

Darren was really fired up now. His face was red with anger and although Jess was trying to get him to sit back down, he shook her hand off.

'You've had it in for us since the beginning,' he yelled at Katherine. 'Well I'll tell you this much. You ain't having our baby.'

'Darren, calm down,' I told him.

My heart was pounding. I could see he was furious, and I was genuinely worried about what he was going to do next. All the shouting had woken Jimmy up and he started to stir in the corner. This really wasn't helping their case.

I'd painted a picture of these devoted teenage parents trying to do their best for their son despite their difficult upbringing, and he was destroying everything I'd said. I could see Jess was embarrassed that he was making a scene.

'Come on, Daz,' she pleaded. 'This ain't going to help us. Sit back down and we can talk about it.'

She put her hand on his arm in an effort to try and soothe him but he brushed her away again.

'I ain't standing for this,' he said. 'Let's get out of here.'

He grabbed Jess's hand, pulled her up and the two of them walked out. I got up and went and checked on Jimmy but thankfully he had settled himself back to sleep.

'It's typical teenage, hot-headed, impulsive behaviour,' said Katherine. 'This is why I don't think either of them are mature enough to be parents.'

Jess and Darren really were playing right into her hands. I felt so frustrated and disappointed.

'Would it be all right if I nipped out quickly to check they're both OK?' I asked.

'Yes, of course,' said Katherine.

'Could you please keep an eye on Jimmy for me?' I asked Becky before I went out.

I found them both outside. Darren was pacing up and down the pavement and was still absolutely livid.

'Who does she think she is?' he raged. 'We love our baby. Why do we have to prove anything to her?'

Whereas Darren was angry, Jess was very tearful and worried.

'Why's she doing this to us, Maggie?' she sobbed. 'What happens at the end of the six weeks? What if we don't pass? Why can't she just come round to your house and watch us there? I don't want to go to no family centre.'

'I know you're both cross and worried, but storming out of a meeting isn't the answer,' I told them. 'Calm down and come back in with me.'

'No way,' said Darren. 'I ain't being in the same room as that woman no more. I'm off home.'

I could tell that Jess was torn about whether to stay or go with him.

'Jess,' I said, 'come back into the meeting, otherwise it's more evidence of your lack of commitment.'

'OK,' she sighed.

Darren still refused point-blank, but I was relieved that Jess at least showed willing.

When we walked back in, Katherine had obviously called a break as everyone was standing around having a cup of tea.

'Right then, shall we continue?' she said when she saw Jess.

'Is Darren coming back in?' asked Kimberly.

Jess shook her head. I could tell that she was close to tears. Her loyalties were split between her boyfriend and wanting to give a good impression in front of Social Services.

'He's still fuming, so I said it's best if he stays outside and I'll tell him what's happened later,' she replied, sounding like she was carrying the weight of the world on her shoulders.

Next it was Kimberly's turn to address the meeting.

'I spoke to Jess at length the other day, and she told me how she very much wanted to be together with Darren and Jimmy and for them to be a family and possibly get their own place.

'I also had a look at the health visitor's report and she says that Jimmy is thriving and is a happy, responsive baby who's putting on weight. So well done to Jess.'

I caught Jess's eye and smiled. She gave me a weak smile back.

'OK then,' said Katherine. 'I will confirm a start date for the family centre assessment to begin and I'll let Maggie and Jess know. Do you want me to pass that information on to Darren too?' she asked.

'It's all right,' scowled Jess. 'I'll tell him.'

When we came out of the meeting, there was no sign of Darren.

'He must have gone home,' sighed Jess, looking disappointed that he hadn't stayed to find out how it had gone. I was annoyed with him for not sticking around and supporting her.

On the drive home, I tried to reassure her about the family centre.

'Just go along with it,' I said. 'Do whatever Katherine has requested and she'll soon see for herself that you're good parents, and it will be fine.

'If Social Services are going to support you to be together as a family and find you somewhere to live, then you need them on your side.'

I didn't tell Jess this, but I could see why Katherine had asked for this assessment. I'd constantly been telling her how well they were doing, but I understood that she needed more people to see them with the baby to back up what I was saying.

'Darren's got to think before he reacts,' I said. 'Shouting and screaming and storming out of meetings isn't going to do you any favours or solve anything – it's just going to get Katherine's back up.'

'I know,' she said. 'He just gets really angry when they're slagging us off.'

At least Jess was more rational when Darren wasn't around. She was very quiet for the rest of the day and I could tell she was worried about the family centre. I did my best to reassure her.

The following day she was changing Jimmy's nappy in her bedroom when I went to talk to her.

'Are you OK?' I asked. 'You've been very quiet since we came home yesterday.'

'I'm scared, Maggie,' she said, her voice quivering with emotion. 'What if we mess up at the family centre and do something wrong? Katherine's out to get us, you know that.'

I watched as she expertly put a new nappy on Jimmy and blew a raspberry on his tummy. He cooed and kicked his legs in delight and she gave him a big smile. It was reassuring to see her happy and interacting so naturally with her baby. I could only hope that she would feel relaxed enough to demonstrate the same skills at the family centre.

'Jess, look at you,' I said. 'You're a good mum. You know how to look after Jimmy.'

'I'm trying my hardest,' she sighed. 'Not that anyone has noticed.'

'I've noticed,' I said. 'I know it's hard, but try and look at the family centre as a positive thing. I've had lots of parents who've had to go to these centres and they've really appreciated the support. Sometimes they've even asked for it.

'As well as observing you, they teach you things like how to wean Jimmy when he's old enough to start eating food, and they might show you different ways you can play with him to encourage his development.'

'But you can teach me all that,' she said.

I really felt for her, and I was secretly worried about how this was going to play out. The truth of it was that being assessed at a family centre generally either makes or breaks people. It would quickly show Jess and Darren's commitment to their baby – their ability to turn up on time three days a week, seeing how they responded to Jimmy and his needs. They'd be continually observed.

The sessions were due to start a couple of days later. Jess hardly slept the night before, she was so nervous about it.

'Be how you are here with Jimmy and you'll be absolutely fine,' I told her.

'I just hope Daz shows up,' she said. 'He's still so angry about it.'

A support worker came and collected her at 8.45 a.m. She went straight to Darren's afterwards, so I didn't see her until later on that evening. I was on tenterhooks all day, wondering how it had gone.

'Well?' I asked. 'How was it?'

'OK, I suppose,' she said.

She described how the centre was like a little self-contained flat within a Social Services office.

'There was a bedroom with a cot in it so we could put Jimmy down for a nap if he needed one, and a little kitchen where we could make a cup of tea,' she said.

'What did you have to do?'

'There were loads of baby toys out and they watched us play with Jimmy for a bit,' she said. 'You'd have been proud of me, Maggie, I read him a story.'

'Really?' I laughed. 'You read him a book out loud?'

'Yep,' she said. 'I did. Darren thought I was mad but I was determined they were gonna write something good about us.'

'Well done for doing something out of your comfort zone,' I said. 'What about Darren?' I asked. 'How did he cope with it all?'

79

'He was OK,' she said. 'It was dead weird with these two women watching everything we did, but they was nice to us and Daz didn't lose it or go off on one.'

It was a relief for me to hear that he'd turned up and managed to keep it together, and it restored my faith in Darren.

I knew it was hard work for Jess getting Jimmy dressed and ready to be out the door by 8.45 a.m three times a week. It was always a rush, and I tried to help wherever I could by giving Jimmy his bottle while she had a shower and making her breakfast.

I didn't know how it was going as the support workers didn't say anything on a morning when they picked Jess up. I could only go on what she had told me.

My phone rang one morning, and it was one of the support workers from the family centre.

'Would you mind reminding Jess to bring some nappies in with her when she comes tomorrow, please?' she asked. 'She used all ours up yesterday and she didn't bring any again today.'

'Yes, no problem,' I said.

Jess was upset when she came home that night.

'I got into trouble today because I didn't bring no clean nappies for Jimmy,' she said. 'I just forgot.'

'I know,' I told her. 'They rang me about it. Don't worry,' I said. 'Everybody forgets things from time to time.'

I went through the nappy bag with her that night. There were a couple of mouldy bottles in there and a dirty nappy festering at the bottom.

'Jess, you've got to take responsibility and keep this clean,' I said. 'On a morning, check it before you go. You need nappies, milk, bottles, cotton wool and a change of clothes.'

'Why do I need a change of clothes?' she asked.

'Not for you, silly,' I said. 'For Jimmy.'

The second week, the support worker called again.

'I wanted to let you know that mum had a bit of a hard morning,' she said.

My heart sank.

'Oh, no,' I said. 'What happened?'

'The baby was very grizzly today and he wouldn't settle for his morning nap. I think she was finding it very difficult and in the end she burst into tears. She popped out for a quick break and she came back half an hour later.'

'How was she when she got back?'

'OK, I think,' she said. 'We helped dad get the baby settled and he was fine in the end.'

'Thanks for the heads-up,' I said.

Jess had already gone to Darren's, so I didn't want to ring her. I had to wait until she came home that evening to talk to her.

'So how was today?' I asked casually.

She took one look at me and burst into tears.

'Hey,' I said, putting my arm around her. 'It can't be that bad.'

'It was,' she snivelled. 'Jimmy wouldn't go down for his nap and he was crying and crying but I couldn't settle him and he wouldn't stop.

'The workers were looking at me and the more I panicked, the more hysterical he was getting. In the end I couldn't take no more – I walked out.'

'How long were you gone for?' I asked.

'Half an hour,' she said. 'I went outside and had a cry. I knew Jimmy would be OK cos Daz was there.'

I thought it was quite a long time to have been away from the centre, although I didn't say anything.

'We all have bad days, and often babies won't do what we want them to,' I soothed. 'Unfortunately your bad day happened when you had a team of people looking over your shoulder, checking up on you.'

I hoped Jess could move on from this and not crumble under the pressure, but I wasn't so sure.

SEVEN

A Bombshell

Three weeks into the assessment and the pressure was definitely getting to Jess and Darren. Katherine called one morning and I could tell she wasn't happy.

'I'm worried, Maggie,' she said. 'Things have started to slip.'

'What sort of things?' I asked.

'Like Jess continually turning up without the basics that she needs for Jimmy such as nappies, milk, a spare change of clothes. You do have an adequate supply of nappies and formula at home that Jess can use for the baby?'

'Of course I do,' I said, peeved that she would even question such a thing. 'I'm always reminding her to make sure she's got everything that she needs in her change bag.'

Admittedly it wasn't good that Jess was being so disorganised, but I didn't think it was the end of the world. I'd just have to have another word with her about going through her bag on a morning. But there was worse to come.

'Did you know Darren's not bothered to turn up at the family centre for the past couple of sessions?' Katherine told me.

My heart sank.

'No, I didn't know that,' I said. 'How come?'

'Jess told the support workers that he was ill, and then later on they heard her on the phone to him asking if he'd had a nice lie-in and then chatting to him about how he'd gone with his brother to buy a car.'

Oh, Jess, I thought. *What's going on? Why are you being so naive?*

All these silly choices meant that everything was stacking up against them.

'Is she still coming in on time on an evening?' Katherine asked.

'Yes,' I said. 'Give or take five or ten minutes here and there.'

'Well, at least that's one positive,' she said.

Katherine suggested I went through the baby bag with Jess every night to check that she'd got everything.

'We did do this for a while until she assured me she was responsible enough to do it on her own,' I said. 'I'll have a word with her about being more organised and I'll also drop a few packets of nappies and a tin of formula up to the family centre when I'm next passing, just in case.'

'Thanks,' said Katherine. 'I'll be talking to Darren *again* about the importance of this assessment.'

When I put the phone down I was still reeling about the fact that Darren hadn't bothered to turn up, and that Jess was clearly making excuses for him. The assessment was for both of them together to prove their commitment to Jimmy. Not turning up didn't do anything to help their case.

When Jess got back that evening, I was waiting to have a chat with her.

'I heard from Katherine today,' I told her.

'Oh yeah?' she said. 'What did she want?'

'She wants me to make sure that you're a bit better organised with putting things in the nappy bag for Jimmy. I was thinking we could have a star chart, like we do for the steriliser, so you can mark each item off that you know you need.'

'OK,' she sighed. 'I don't see what the big deal is. It's a few nappies and bit of milk.'

'It's about you proving that you're able to meet Jimmy's needs, and if you haven't got any clean nappies for him and milk to feed him with then you can't do that. So, how's Darren finding it?' I asked casually.

'Oh, I think we're both in a bit of trouble there,' she said. 'Daz didn't come for two days and I said he was ill but then the lady heard me on the phone talking about him going out with his brother and she knew that he'd lied.'

'So he wasn't poorly?' I asked.

'Nah,' said Jess. 'Just a bit tired and fed up.'

'Jess, I can't believe you're being so naive,' I said.

It was so frustrating. I'd worked so hard to support them both, fight their corner with Social Services and help them every step of the way. Yet they weren't helping themselves.

'Of course she's going to be listening in if you're silly enough to have that conversation right in front of her. What are you and Darren playing at? You can't be telling lies for him. If you want to be together and be a family, this isn't a good way of showing your commitment to Jimmy, is it?'

'I know,' she said. 'It's just that he's finding it really hard, always being watched and everybody checking up on us all the time.'

'But if he wants you all to be a family then I'm afraid that's what he has to do,' I said. 'It's not for ever, but if he keeps missing sessions that doesn't look good.'

'I know, I know,' she said. 'I'll talk to him.'

I was so disappointed and frustrated with them both. I felt like I was banging my head against a brick wall.

The following day I made sure I was up early enough to go through the nappy bag with Jess to check that she'd got everything.

'Don't worry, I spoke to Daz last night and he's definitely coming to the family centre today,' she told me.

'Good,' I said. 'I'll see you both back here for tea later.'

I knew Katherine had already spoken to Darren, but I didn't think it would do any harm to reiterate what she'd said when he came round that night.

'Katherine said you missed a couple of days at the family centre this week,' I said to him.

'Yeah,' he sighed. 'I was poorly.'

'It's a pity you weren't poorly enough to stay in bed rather than go off looking for cars with your brother then,' I said.

Darren blushed. 'Oh, er, yeah. Sorry,' he muttered.

'So is looking at cars more important to you than seeing your son?' I asked.

'No, it ain't,' he said.

'Well, that's what those support workers think, and that's exactly what they'll be writing down in their reports.'

'I said I'm sorry,' he said sheepishly.

'There's no point apologising to me,' I said. 'It's not me making an assessment on your parenting. Darren, you've got to buck your ideas up.'

'I will,' he promised, but I wasn't sure in all honesty whether he appreciated how serious it was.

In our house I'm a big believer in everyone mucking in and doing chores. If I cook, I expect a hand afterwards with the clearing up. So when we'd finished eating, I held Jimmy while Louisa, Lily, Jess and Darren did the washing-up. They were larking around and Darren was flicking washing-up bubbles at the girls and they were all screeching with laughter and whacking him with tea towels. As I sat at the kitchen table and watched them messing about, it suddenly struck me how young Jess and Darren were. They were still kids. They might have been parents themselves, but they still needed to be parented.

Ever since Jess had come to live with me I'd always been their biggest supporter, telling Katherine what a strong relationship they had and how they would make good, responsible parents to Jimmy despite their age. But after the past few weeks, doubts were starting to creep in. Had I got it wrong? Could they actually do this? The one thing I was sure of was that they loved Jimmy, but was that enough? Were they, as Social Services seemed to think, too young?

I could hardly sleep that night worrying about it, but the next day I felt a lot more positive. Jess was trying so hard to be on top of things. She'd got up extra early that morning to go through the nappy bag and check she'd got everything, and she proudly showed it to me before she left.

'I've not forgotten nothing,' she said.

'Well done,' I told her. 'Katherine will have nothing to complain about.'

When she left, I rang Becky to talk through my concerns.

'With Darren not turning up, I started to worry that I'd got this really wrong,' I said.

'Of course Darren and Jess are going to have wobbles every now and again,' said Becky. 'We both know the family centre is a high-pressure environment. It's stressful for people, no matter what their age, being watched like that all the time. Do you know any mothers who are perfect and get it right all the time?'

'No,' I said. 'You're right.'

They both loved Jimmy, and with the right support and guidance I still believed that they could be good parents. My gut was telling me I couldn't give up on them now.

Chatting to Becky had reassured me. Until later that evening, when my phone beeped with a text from Jess. It was 6.45 p.m., and she should have been on her way back from Darren's by now.

Missed bus. Going 2 get next one.

I messaged her straight back.

OK. See u soon.

I knew her buses were every fifteen minutes, so even if she'd missed one she'd be back by 7.30 p.m. at the very latest. However, by eight there was still no sign of her and Jimmy.

'Is Jess late home?' sighed Lily as I tucked her in. 'Katherine's not going to be happy.'

Even a seven-year-old understood that this wasn't good behaviour.

When I came downstairs there was another text.

Bus didn't stop. Waiting 4 next one.

I was fuming. Did Jess think I was born yesterday? She could have caught four or five buses by now, and I suspected she was sitting on the sofa at Darren's. I had no doubt she was trying it on.

Whatever the reason if u r not back by 9 then I have to report u missing to the police, I typed.

I didn't hear anything after that.

'Do you want me to wait up with you?' asked Louisa.

'No, it's OK, sweetheart,' I said. 'I'm more cross than worried. She'll show her face soon enough.'

At 9 p.m. I rang the duty worker at my agency. I explained that I'd been in text contact with Jess but that she hadn't come home and was now two hours late. As I was chatting, I heard a faint knock at the front door.

'Oh, hold on,' I said. 'I think that's her, but I'll ring you back if it's not.'

I ran to the front door and opened it to find a sheepish-looking Jess standing there with Jimmy asleep in the buggy. I could tell by her face that she knew she'd messed up.

'Why are you so late?' I asked her.

'I told you in the texts,' she said. 'Now Daz can't drive me I have to get the bus. I missed one, one didn't stop then there was no more for ages.'

'Jess, do you think I'm stupid?' I said. 'That was over two hours ago. I know when someone's messing me about and telling fibs. What's really going on?'

She looked down at the ground and refused to make eye contact with me.

'I didn't want to leave him. It's so hard having to get Jimmy in the buggy and go out there in the dark. I'm fed up of it. Why can't I stay with Darren? It's not fair.'

'You know why,' I sighed. 'I've told you enough times.'

I felt like a broken record – I was saying the same things over and over again but Jess still wasn't listening.

The following night was the final straw. Seven came and went and there was no sign of Jess or Jimmy. I tried calling her mobile and texting but heard nothing.

At 8 p.m. I phoned my agency for advice.

'Give it another hour, then call it in to the police,' a duty worker told me.

My patience had well and truly run out. At 9 p.m. on the dot, heart sinking, I picked up the phone and reported Jess and Jimmy missing.

It was 10.30 p.m. before two police officers came round to get some details. They were in the middle of taking down a description when Jess finally turned up with Jimmy asleep in his buggy. As I opened the door to her, she looked at me with a mixture of shame and impertinence.

'Come in,' I said matter-of-factly. 'The police are here.'

'But I . . .'

'Save it, Jess,' I snapped. 'I don't want to hear your excuses. The officers want to have a word with you.'

We left Jimmy asleep in his buggy in the hallway and I led her into the living room. Jess sat down meekly on the settee, not making eye contact with the two officers.

'We're glad you're back safely but you've wasted our time,' one of them told her. 'Why didn't you answer your phone and let your foster carer know where you were?'

'I didn't hear it,' she said.

'You need to stick to arrangements,' the other officer told her. 'You can't be out until all hours of the night with a baby and not let anyone know. What's your social worker going to say about this?'

Jess shrugged. 'She ain't going to be pleased,' she said quietly.

'I'm not surprised,' the officer told her. 'We're going to leave now so you can all get some sleep, but if this happens again we're not going to be very happy. Do you understand?'

Jess nodded. She looked like she was about to burst into tears.

After the police had gone, I started locking up. Thankfully Jimmy was still fast asleep. I started unbuckling him from the buggy and unzipped his coat.

'Aren't you going to tell me off or ask me where I was?' said Jess.

'I'm fed up with hearing your excuses, and I'm not going to waste my breath telling you off,' I said, gently lifting Jimmy out of the pushchair. 'I'm going to bed, and I think you and Jimmy should do the same.'

I handed her the baby and he began to wriggle around in her arms.

'You'll need to give him a nappy change and get him into his pyjamas before you put him down,' I told her.

'OK.' She shrugged. 'Do you want to give him a kiss good-night?' she asked.

'Get him changed and settled in the cot and I'll come in and see him,' I said.

I knew this was more about her wanting reassurance than anything to do with Jimmy.

When I came into her bedroom, Jess was sitting on the bed. 'He's fast asleep,' she said.

'So he should be at this time of night,' I told her.

I went over to the cot and kissed his cheek.

'Maggie, I really am sorry, you know,' said Jess meekly.

I was so frustrated with her. I knew she loved her son, yet my patience was wearing thin with the constant battle to get her to stick to Katherine's rules. I didn't know how much more of this I could take.

'You might be sorry, but at the end of the day your actions are going to have consequences,' I said. 'And when those consequences come you can't say I haven't warned you. Now night-night.'

I wasn't going to pussyfoot around her any more. She needed to know the truth and prepare herself for what was going to happen next.

I'm not one to bear a grudge, and I don't believe in carrying arguments over to the next morning. All it does is create a bad atmosphere in the house for the other children. Jess knew she'd messed up, so there was no point me going on and on about it because I'd said my piece the night before.

I could tell she was worried that I was angry with her as she was tiptoeing around me.

'Maggie, would it be OK for you to give Jimmy his bottle while I go and get ready?' she asked meekly.

'Yes, of course,' I said. 'How did you sleep last night?'

'Not very well,' she said. 'I kept on thinking about things and worrying. What do you think Katherine's going to say?'

'You know Katherine as well as I do,' I told her. 'What do you think she's going to say?'

'I think she's going to be cross. She's had it in for us since day one anyway.'

'Jess, I think Katherine's patience is running out, just like mine is. She's given you lots of chances, but every time you've let us down.'

The support worker came to pick her up as usual and at 9.30 a.m. Katherine phoned.

'Enough's enough,' she said. 'I'm fed up with this persistent negative behaviour. I've just heard that Darren's not turned up to the family centre again today and Jess has been back late two nights in a row.

'The bottom line is we can't have Jimmy being disrupted like this. He needs routine and consistency, not two parents who think they can do whatever the heck they want when they want.

'We can't have a nine-week-old baby being kept out until all hours of the night and us not knowing where he is.'

The sad fact was I completely agreed with her, and there was nothing I could say in Jess's defence.

'So what's going to happen now?' I asked.

'I've talked to my manager, and at 11 a.m. we're going to hold a child protection meeting where I'm going to suggest that we go for an Emergency Protection Order on Jimmy,' she said.

An Emergency Protection Order, or an EPO as it's known, meant that Jimmy was being taken into the care system and Jess no longer had full parental responsibility over him. It was a short-term measure put in place to protect a child who was considered to be at risk until enough evidence had been gathered to apply to the courts to get an Interim Care Order (ICO), if that was what Social Services decided to do.

'I understand,' I said. 'What about Jess? When are you thinking of telling her?'

'Instead of going round to Darren's after the family centre today, I'm going to get the support worker to drop her back at your house and I'll come round and talk to her. How do you think she'll take it?' asked Katherine.

'I think she'll be absolutely devastated,' I said.

'Well, I can't believe she didn't see this coming after all the warnings she's had,' she told me. 'They've left us with no choice. This is the way it has to go.'

After I'd put the phone down, I rang Becky to tell her the news.

'How do you feel about it?' she asked.

'I know it's the right thing to do but I still feel very sad,' I said. 'I'm sad for Jess and Darren that it's come to this, and also I'm worried about how they're going to react. They're not going to take it well, especially Darren.'

'That's not our concern,' Becky told me. 'Katherine will need to sort that out. I'm assuming she'll go and talk to him after she's spoken to Jess.'

Becky also wanted to check that I was happy to foster Jimmy as well as Jess.

'Of course I'll take him,' I said. 'He's here anyway, and it's so much better to keep him and Jess together.'

All morning I was walking around with a knot in my stomach, dreading Jess coming back. I knew she wouldn't be happy that she was being brought to my house rather than being allowed to go to Darren's for the afternoon. The support worker dropped her off just before lunch.

'It's so unfair,' she grumbled. 'They told me I had to come back here and not go to Darren's cos that bloody Katherine wants to see me. She just wants to have a go at me about last night, doesn't she? Well, she can do that any time.'

The hard thing was I couldn't tell her what was happening. I did feel guilty but I knew I had to stick to the rules, and it wasn't my place to pass on news like this. This was Social

Service's decision, and as her social worker, it was down to Katherine to tell her.

'You're probably right,' I said. 'I'm sure she wants to have a word with you about last night. While we're waiting, shall we have some lunch? You must be hungry.'

It wasn't appropriate for me to say anything and break such devastating news to her. I'd be there to help her with any questions she might have and to pick up the pieces afterwards. I really felt for her as I knew what anger, upset and frustration this was going to cause.

Katherine arrived just as we'd finished our ham sandwiches. Typically of her, she got straight to the point.

'Jess, we're not happy with the way things are going,' she said. 'We've asked you to co-operate with us via the contract, but lately you haven't been sticking to the terms of that contract. You've been continually late and Maggie has had to involve the police on numerous occasions.'

'I'm sorry about last night,' said Jess. 'I'll try harder. I promise I will.'

'It's not just about last night. We've given you countless chances, but the fact is you're not listening,' she continued. 'You don't seem to care that your baby is out at all times of night when he should be settled in his bed. You turn up at the family centre with no nappies or milk, so how do we know he's getting changed and fed?'

'But you know he's OK,' said Jess. 'He's happy and healthy. I ain't hurt him or nothing.'

'I'm afraid it's too late and you've left us with no choice,' Katherine told her. 'We feel that Jimmy is potentially at risk, so this morning we applied to the family court for an Emergency Protection Order on him.'

'A what?' she gasped. 'What does that mean? What's a protection order?

'You're not taking away my baby,' she screamed. 'I'll die if you take away my baby.'

She burst into tears, threw her head down on the table and started to sob. She was crying so much, she started to hyperventilate.

'Come on, Jess, take deep breaths,' I said, rubbing her back. 'Calm down and listen to Katherine and she'll explain it to you.'

'It means that we don't feel that Jimmy's needs are being met and prioritised in your care, so he's now in the care of the local authority,' Katherine told her.

'No!' sobbed Jess. 'You can't take him away from me. I love him.'

'Jess, listen to me,' I urged. 'Jimmy's not being taken away from you.'

'What does it mean then?' she whimpered.

'It means that Jimmy's being taken into the care system, like you, but he can stay here and he can still sleep in your room and you can still feed him and look after him and be his mummy,' I said. 'What it does mean is that Jimmy can't leave the placement without me.'

'So I can't take him to Darren's?' she asked.

'No, I'm afraid not,' I said. 'He has to be with me at all times.'

'We'd still like you and Darren to continue having your sessions at the family centre with Jimmy,' said Katherine.

'What's the f***ing point?' she sobbed, tears streaming down her face. 'You've already decided you're taking him away from us. Why are you doing this?'

'Because you didn't do as we asked and continually broke your contract,' said Katherine. 'You've been in the placement nine weeks and we're still having the same problems. You can remain here with Maggie, but if you're going to be difficult about it then we can arrange for Jimmy to be fostered elsewhere if that's what you want.'

Jess shook her head. 'No,' she sobbed. 'I don't want that. I want him to be here with me. Please don't send him somewhere else.'

'Once the court has issued the paperwork and a judge has signed it, I'll bring it straight round here later today,' she said.

'Don't bother,' snapped Jess. 'I don't want it and I don't wanna see you.'

She started to cry again. I took Katherine to one side.

'It's OK,' I told her. 'You go. I'll talk to Jess and try and calm her down and answer her questions.'

'Thanks,' said Katherine. 'I need to go and talk to Darren now.'

'Good luck,' I said, because I knew she was certainly going to need it. Jess was devastated, but Darren was going to hit the roof.

Jess sat at the kitchen table, shell-shocked, as the enormity of what had happened sank in.

'Why are they doing this to us, Maggie?' she asked. 'Does this mean we're never going to get Jimmy back? That they're never, ever going to let us be a family?'

'No, it doesn't mean that,' I reassured her. 'They're still carrying on your assessment, which is a good sign. You've got seven days to prove to them that you're committed to your baby and you want to work with them before they go for an Interim Care Order.'

However, I knew in my heart that although it wouldn't destroy their chances of becoming the family they so wanted, it would make things a lot harder. I also knew that EPOs were often the start of a process that ended up with adoption. If they wanted to keep Jimmy, this pair of teenagers was facing one heck of a fight. I just hoped they had it in them.

EIGHT

Fight or Flight

An hour after Katherine had left, Jess's mobile rang.

'It's Darren,' she said, jumping up.

She answered it and walked off into the other room.

'You've got to calm down,' I heard her say to him. 'It's OK. It don't mean they're taking Jimmy away. Maggie explained it to me.

'Daz, listen to me, please,' she begged, her voice rising to be heard.

When she came back in, she looked worried.

'Katherine's told him and he's going mental,' she said. 'He wants to go up to Social Services to have it out with them but I told him not to as it would only make things worse. I need to go and see him, Maggie,' she said. 'I'm worried about what he's gonna do.'

'Well, it's only Jimmy who has to stay here with me,' I said. 'So why don't you go round to see Darren and have a chat to him?'

'Ta,' she said. 'What time am I allowed to stay out until?'

'I'd like you back for seven as normal,' I said. 'Jimmy's still your baby, so you need to be back here to give him a bath and put him to bed.'

99

'OK,' she said. 'Thanks, Maggie.'

Despite all of their silly games, I really felt for them. At times like this I could see Jess's childlike vulnerability. They were both terrified, and still didn't quite understand what today's developments meant.

While Jess went to see Darren, I had a quiet afternoon at home with Jimmy. I read him stories, put him on his play mat and gave him a bath. It was what we both needed after the roller coaster of the past few days. I sat on the sofa with him and he cuddled into me as I gave him a bottle. As he sucked away, he gazed up at me with his big blue eyes.

'You're such a good little boy, aren't you?' I smiled at him and he gave me a lovely gummy grin back.

All this drama was going on around him, but thankfully he seemed happy enough. At the end of the day, what really mattered was him and his welfare. When Lily came back from school, she was delighted to find the baby there for once.

I kept every case confidential, and I wasn't going to share with her and Louisa the ins and outs of what was happening with Jess, but I felt it was important for them to know that things had changed slightly.

'You're going to be seeing a lot more of Jimmy from now on,' I told them both. 'He has to stay with me now rather than Jess. So if you ever see Jess and Jimmy heading out of the door together without me, then you need to tell me.'

'Oh goody,' said Lily. 'That means I'll be able to play with him more and cuddle him.'

'As long as you're gentle.' I smiled.

When Louisa and I were together in the kitchen later she talked to me about Jess.

'Does this mean Jimmy's going to be adopted?'

'I don't honestly know, love,' I said.

'I'd really appreciate it, though, if you could be a little less hard on Jess,' I told her. 'She's going through a difficult time, and I don't think all your childcare advice is helpful.'

'I'm only passing on what I learn at college,' she said.

'I know you're only trying to help, love, but at the end of the day being a mother is hard, and being a mother in the care system is even harder.'

'OK,' she sighed. 'I was just trying to be nice.'

'I know, but sometimes that can come across as a bit bossy and condescending,' I said. 'Jess needs all our support at the minute as she's feeling very lost.'

Just after tea, the phone rang. It was Jess.

'I'm on my way back,' she said. 'Could I bring Darren with me, Maggie? He needs to talk to you. He wants you to explain everything like you did to me.'

'OK,' I said.

Because circumstances had changed and his visit hadn't been prearranged, while they were on their way round I quickly phoned a duty worker at my fostering agency.

'I'm ringing to let you know that I've agreed for Darren to come round tonight for a couple of hours,' I said. 'They're both very upset and scared after today's news, and they want to talk things through with me.

'Jimmy and Lily will be in bed and Louisa's going to a friend's house, so we'll have peace and quiet.'

'That's OK,' she said. 'Thanks for letting us know. We'll make sure that Social Services are informed. Remember to record it in your own notes too.'

'I will do,' I said.

When Darren and Jess arrived, they looked wrung out and exhausted. I could tell by their bloodshot eyes that they'd both been crying.

'Are you OK, Darren?' I asked.

'I've just got a bit of a cold,' he sniffed, refusing to make eye contact with me.

He was still very angry.

'I went off on one when that Katherine told me about that order thing,' he said. 'She says she's going to meet us at the family centre on Monday morning and tell me when I can see Jimmy. She says I can't come round here for tea no more, and when I see Jimmy it has to be with people from Social Services.'

Hearing this, I was worried that I was going to get into trouble for letting him come round tonight so I was relieved that I'd made that call to my agency.

Seeing them so upset made me feel sad and frustrated. Neither of them could understand how it had come to this. At the end of the day, they were two kids who were all alone in the world. No one was supporting them or fighting for them. All they had was each other.

'Have you talked to your mum about what's happened?' I asked Darren.

His eyes filled with tears.

'She said it was better sooner rather than later that Jimmy was taken off us and adopted out.'

'Have you had any contact with your mum, Jess?'

She laughed.

'There's no point,' she sighed. 'She don't care what happens to me. She's made it very clear she's washed her hands of me and that she thinks I'm scum.'

I made them a cup of tea and some sandwiches and sat with them at the kitchen table. All I could do was listen and answer any questions they might have.

'Can we stop them doing this, Maggie?' asked Darren. 'Can we just say Jess will sign another contract and we promise to stick to it?'

'I'm afraid it doesn't work like that,' I told him. 'This order is Social Services' way of saying that they're worried about Jimmy. They don't feel that you've been listening to them, and this is their way of making you listen.

'A nine-week-old baby can't be out at all times of night with no one knowing where he is. Social Services very rightly is not prepared to take that risk on a baby so young.'

I explained to them that an EPO lasted seven days and then Social Services would have to tell them what they were doing next.

'Darren, arrangements are likely to be a lot more formal now about you seeing Jimmy,' I said. 'Katherine will tell you when and where contact will take place.'

'Well, it sounds like there ain't no point in me seeing him,' he said. 'If he's gonna be taken away from us I don't want to see him no more.'

Jess started to cry.

'Daz, you can't say that,' she sobbed. 'Course you want to see your baby. He's our little boy.'

'You're only saying this because you're in shock and you're angry,' I said. 'Nobody is taking Jimmy away from you. They're just saying that they want you to follow the rules. It's the weekend now, but let's see what happens on Monday and what Katherine says.'

Their heads were spinning, and I could see they were exhausted after the day's events.

'Darren, you need to be going now,' I told him.

'Before I leave, can I go and see my son and kiss him goodbye?' he asked.

'It's late and he's fast asleep,' I said.

'Please, Maggie,' he begged. 'I don't know when I'm going to be allowed to see him next.'

'OK,' I said. 'I'll take you up, but try not to wake him.'

I led Darren upstairs and waited in the doorway of the bedroom. I watched as he leant over the cot and kissed Jimmy gently on the forehead.

'I love you so much, and I'm sorry we've let you down,' he whispered. 'Bye-bye, son.'

Tears pricked my eyes as I watched this young lad being so tender towards his baby. Despite how he and Jess had behaved, I knew that deep down Darren loved this little boy, and I could see he was slowly realising that they could lose him. As he walked away, he buried his head in his hands and started to cry. Seeing this seventeen-year-old lad sobbing like a baby made me realise how vulnerable he was too.

'Don't tell Jess about this,' he said, wiping his face with his tracksuit top. 'I have to stay strong for her.'

The pair of them clung to each other in the hallway as they said goodbye.

'I just want us to be a family,' she said.

'I know,' he told her, stroking her hair. 'And we will be one day. It's gonna be OK.'

When Darren had left, I suggested that Jess go up to bed.

'It's been a long day,' I told her. 'We all need to get some sleep.'

I had a soak in the bath and as I passed Jess's bedroom, I knocked gently on her door. She wasn't asleep yet.

'Come in,' she called.

'There's one thing I forgot to mention,' I said. 'Now Jimmy's in my care, before I go to bed I'd like to have a little peep at him and check that he's OK. I'm not doubting your abilities for one minute – it's just something that I have to do as a foster carer,' I explained.

'I'll always knock on your door, and if you're asleep then I'll just poke my head round and have a quick look at him.'

I could see the cot from the doorway and there was a night light next to it.

Jess nodded.

'Please can he still stay in here with me?' she asked.

'Yes, of course he can,' I said. 'Now you close your eyes and try and get some sleep.'

'I can't,' she said. 'I'm lying here and all I can think about is them taking Jimmy away from me and then I get all panicked and I can't breathe.'

'You need to try,' I said. 'There's nothing you can do about it tonight. Get some rest and let's see what tomorrow brings.'

'OK, I'll try,' she said. 'Thanks, Maggie, for helping us and for letting Darren come round.'

I was exhausted too, but, like Jess, I had trouble sleeping as thoughts whirred around my head. I couldn't stop thinking about Darren and Jess and how sad and frightened they'd been today hearing about the EPO. After tossing and turning for a couple of hours, I decided to get up and make a cup of tea. I turned on my computer and started writing down my records about what had happened that evening. Sometimes I find that getting my thoughts down clears my head and helps me sleep. Thankfully it did the trick, and as soon as my head hit the pillow again, I finally dozed off.

The following day was a Saturday, so I didn't have to rush out on the school run. Jess had been up early with Jimmy and was looking tired and washed out. Lily and Louisa, meanwhile, were begging me to take them to the local shopping centre.

'I'll have to take Jimmy with me, so why don't you come too?' I asked Jess.

'OK,' she sighed.

However, as we walked around the shops she seemed to be dragging her feet and was very quiet.

'Can I go and see Darren now?' she asked after about half an hour.

I couldn't believe what I was hearing. After everything that had happened, I thought she would be desperate to spend time with Jimmy and prove her commitment to him rather than sloping off to Darren's at every available opportunity.

'Jess, think how that looks,' I told her. 'You should be spending the day with your baby.'

'But he'll be fine with you,' she said. 'I've seen him this morning and I'll see him tonight. I miss Darren so much, and even though Jimmy can't come with me, I can still go.'

Technically she was right. Jimmy would be staying with me, so there was nothing stopping her from going round to Darren's house.

'I'm not happy about you going to Darren's but I can't stop you,' I sighed. 'However, I'd appreciate it if you were back at 7 p.m. to do Jimmy's bath and bed. Remember, you're still in the care system and therefore deemed vulnerable, so if you're not back until late, even if you've not got Jimmy with you, I'll still have to report you as missing to the police.'

'I know,' she snapped.

I hoped she'd got the message, so I was disappointed when she came in just before eight.

'Where's Jimmy?' she asked.

'Jess, he was shattered so I did his bath and put him to bed an hour ago. I can't keep him up waiting for you. You've got to understand that if you come back at this time, you won't see him. You're lucky, as I was about to pick up the phone to ring this in.'

I also needed to pull her up about the state of her room.

'Tomorrow you need to start putting some of Jimmy's clothes away that are scattered all over your floor,' I told her. 'I couldn't tell what was clean and what was dirty when I was in there. There were dirty nappies everywhere too. I spent a good half an hour hunting around for things I needed.

'Jess, if I think your care of Jimmy has deteriorated and your bedroom is not up to scratch, then I'll move him in with me. Do you understand?' I said, and she nodded.

I felt the knot of anxiety tightening in my stomach. I really wasn't sure how this new arrangement was going to work out. I thought it would be the wake-up call that Jess needed, but if anything, her attitude and behaviour were going downhill.

The next morning she came down to breakfast with Jimmy happily nestled in her arms.

'Will you have Jimmy while I go to Darren's?' she asked, passing him to me.

'Jess, you've just got up,' I sighed. 'Don't you at least want to spend a few hours with your baby?'

'I have,' she snapped. 'He's been up since 5.30 a.m. and besides, he's happy with you.'

I wasn't pleased with her spending every day at Darren's, but I knew there was no persuading her.

'You're not going anywhere until you clean your room,' I told her.

She rolled her eyes as I handed her some bin bags and some cleaning wipes.

'I thought you said it was my room and it was my personal space,' she said.

'It is,' I told her. 'But now I have to go in it too, and I don't expect to have to be climbing over piles of dirty nappies.'

In the end she did as I'd asked and cleaned and tidied before she went off to Darren's house. Thankfully that night she was back on time to put Jimmy to bed.

Soon the weekend passed and it was Monday morning. I could tell Jess was nervous about what was going to happen when they met Katherine at the family centre.

'Good luck,' I told her. 'Make sure you listen to what Katherine is telling you and we can talk about it when you get back.'

Just before lunch I saw the support worker's car pull up outside. I was puzzled when I went to answer the door and saw her carrying Jimmy up the path in the car seat.

'Where's Jess?' I asked.

'She went back to Darren's for the day but she said she'd see you later.'

'Oh, OK,' I said.

I was put out that she hadn't come back to chat to me about what had happened. Again, although Jess wasn't breaking any rules by going to Darren's, she just wasn't thinking about the bigger picture and how it looked to Katherine. It didn't say much for her commitment to Jimmy if she was leaving him with me in favour of spending the afternoon with her boyfriend.

'Katherine said to tell you that she'll pop round later on,' the support worker told me, so I knew I wouldn't be kept in the dark for long.

When Katherine arrived she got straight down to business.

'How did it go this morning?' I asked.

'I've had a good talk to the pair of them and told them exactly what's going to happen from now on,' she said. 'I've arranged for them to attend a contact centre for three hours on two afternoons a week so that Darren can see Jimmy and all three of them can be together. They'll still be carrying on with their assessment at the family centre for the other three mornings, and in addition I've asked for a psychological assessment to be carried out on both Jess and Darren.

'At this point it looks like we're going to apply for an Interim Care Order by the end of the week.'

An EPO only lasted for up to seven days, then an ICO took over. Nothing would change if the court granted it and the same rules would still be in place.

'How did Jess and Darren take the news?' I asked.

'As you would expect,' sighed Katherine. 'Shouting and screaming, blaming me and generally not being prepared to listen to anything I was saying.'

'I got a completely different picture when they were here on Friday,' I said. 'They came across as two incredibly sad, scared kids who love their baby and were suddenly facing the realisation that they might lose him.'

'Well that's certainly not the impression they gave me,' huffed Katherine. 'And as for facing up to the fact that they might lose him, Jess has chosen to go back to Darren's house today rather than come back here with Jimmy, which I think speaks volumes to us all about where her priorities truly lie.'

There wasn't much I could say in response to that. It didn't look good, but when it came to Darren, Jess found it impossible to be apart from him.

'I also wanted to remind you about keeping on top of your daily recordings as they could be used in court,' she told me.

'Oh, don't worry, I always do,' I said.

With long-term placements that lasted several months I tended to do weekly recordings, but with this kind of case it was important I kept detailed daily notes.

'Keep it factual,' said Katherine. 'Also please record the amount of time Jess is actually in the placement now and interacting with Jimmy.'

I could see all the evidence was being stacked up against her.

When Jess came back that night, I told her about Katherine's visit.

'How are you feeling about things?' I asked.

'Well, she's already decided from the beginning that this is what's gonna happen,' she said. 'So I was expecting it. There's no point fighting it any more – I know they're gonna be putting Jimmy up for adoption.'

She seemed so defeatist, like all the fight had gone out of her.

'There's a lot of people involved in this case and no one has decided anything yet,' I told her. 'Ultimately that final decision isn't down to Katherine or even Social Services, it's down to a judge in court. Until then you need to do everything you can to co-operate with them.'

Nowadays children who come into the care system have to be dealt with within twenty-six weeks, and that includes any care orders or being placed for adoption. The system has been streamlined to avoid babies and children lingering in care, but at that point, care orders could last months and there was no time frame on anything.

'I'm not sure that you should be going round to Darren's every day,' I told her.

'I'm allowed to,' she snapped. 'Katherine said there's nothing stopping me.'

'Well, yes, she's right,' I said. 'Technically you are allowed to, but think how it looks to Social Services. You're choosing to go to your boyfriend's rather than spend the afternoon caring for your baby. It's giving them a clear indication of where your priorities lie.'

'I ain't doing anything wrong,' she said. 'Darren and me need to be together at the moment. He's still upset about what's happening and things are really difficult.'

I thought she was being incredibly naive. Yes, she was legally allowed to go round to Darren's whenever she wanted as long as Jimmy was with me. However, what she wasn't thinking about was the bigger picture and how it looked to other people, at a time when she should have been going all out to prove her commitment to her son.

But nothing I said seemed to make a blind bit of difference. After the family centre, Jimmy would be brought back to me while Jess went to Darren's. On the days when they had the contact sessions in the afternoons, Jess would spend the mornings with me. When she was with Jimmy, I couldn't fault her parenting. She got up in the night with him and early on a morning and she played and interacted with him.

'They've got such a strong bond and she clearly enjoys being with him,' I told Becky. 'That's why it's such a shame this is happening.'

A couple of days later a judge granted an ICO for Jimmy. That evening a support worker from Social Services rang me.

'Just to let you know that Jess has been in contact with us to tell us that she's staying overnight at Darren's tonight.'

'Oh, OK,' I said, surprised. 'Is she allowed to do that?'

'She's been to see her mum and she's given her permission.'

I was surprised that she'd got her mum involved, but technically Jess was within her rights. Because she was sixteen and had come into care voluntarily, as long as her mum had given permission and Social Services knew where she was so they didn't report her as missing, then that was fine. The rules all concerned Jimmy being in the placement, not her.

I knew she'd obviously phoned them rather than me as she was worried about what I was going to say. While the rules allowed her to do this, she knew my thoughts were that she should be with her baby.

For the next couple of days Jess stayed overnight at Darren's and we didn't see her. According to Katherine, they were both still attending the family centre sessions every morning, and when they went home, a support worker returned Jimmy to me. I moved his Moses basket into my room. For such a young baby he was a good little sleeper, and I must admit it was lovely being woken up on a morning by the sounds of him cooing and gurgling.

I called Becky for a chat.

'I feel like I'm in limbo here,' I said. 'I don't know what this is any more. It's certainly not a mother-and-baby placement as I haven't seen Jess for days. She's not breaking any rules, she's not gone missing and Jimmy is safe with me. I just feel incredibly sad for her that it's come to this.'

'As far as I can see, she's acting like a typical sixteen-year-old,' said Becky. 'She's doing exactly what suits her regardless of the consequences.'

'I can see why she's doing it,' I said. 'She's young and isolated. Darren is the only person in her life who gives her security and support. He *is* her family. What I don't think she realises is the effect that this could have long-term,' I said.

'I certainly get the impression that Katherine is pushing for adoption now,' said Becky.

'Personally I think that's what she's wanted all along, and now Jess is giving her all the evidence she needs,' I sighed.

Lily and Louisa had also noticed Jess wasn't around.

'Where is she?' asked Louisa.

'She's staying with Darren at the minute,' I said.

'For good?' she asked.

'I don't know, sweetheart,' I said. 'I don't know what she's thinking any more.'

One morning, after spending three nights at Darren's, Jess

came back with Jimmy and the support worker after the session at the family centre.

'Ah, hello there, stranger,' I said. 'It's good to see you at last.'

She looked very sheepish and she wouldn't make eye contact with me.

'I've come to get my things, Maggie,' she said. 'I'm moving back in with Darren.'

'Oh no, Jess,' I sighed. 'Please don't do this without understanding how it looks. You're choosing your boyfriend over your baby,' I said. 'You're voting with your feet.'

'That's not true,' she said. 'I love Jimmy with all my heart, you know I do, but I need to be with Darren. I'm fed up of jumping through hoops and going backwards and forwards. I know Jimmy's OK because he'll be with you until we win him back.'

'But don't you see that it will be so much harder for you to convince a court to give you him back if you've chosen not to live in the same place as him?'

Jess shrugged. 'Darren needs me and I need him,' she said.

'What about Jimmy?' I said. 'He needs you too.'

Jess's eyes filled with tears.

'He'll be fine,' she said, her voice wobbling. 'We'll see him at contact.'

I could tell she'd already made her mind up and my pleas were falling on deaf ears.

'Have Social Services even said this is OK?' I asked.

'Yep,' she said. 'I went round to see my mum. She's fed up with the hassle of the police ringing her when I don't turn up, and she said she doesn't want to be bothered by the Social any more so she agreed to ring Katherine and say she don't want me to be in care no more.'

As Jess had been brought in on a voluntary care order she was perfectly within her rights to do that. It was Jimmy they'd been wanting to protect rather than Jess.

'Please think carefully about this,' I urged her.

'I have,' she said. 'And I want to be with Darren. We can see Jimmy every day at the family centre.'

No matter what I said, nothing seemed to make any difference. I sat on her bed holding Jimmy while she packed up her things and tried to squash them into the tiny rucksack she'd arrived with.

'I'll get you a case,' I said as I watched her struggle to fit it all in.

Twenty minutes later she was all packed and ready to go.

'Jess, please make sure you've thought this through properly,' I pleaded. 'I understand you want to be with Darren, but if you do this Social Services are going to see it as yet more evidence of your lack of commitment to your baby.'

She shook her head. 'I have to go,' she said. 'I need to be with Darren.'

However, I could tell by the tears in her eyes and the way she was lingering that she was doing it with a heavy heart.

'Bye-bye, Jim,' she said, bending down and kissing his cheek. 'I love you so much. See you tomorrow. Bye, Maggie.'

'Take care, Jess,' I said. 'You know you can text or call me any time to see how Jimmy is.'

She nodded and looked like she was going to burst into tears.

As the front door closed, my heart felt heavy with sadness and fear. I looked down at the beautiful little baby in my arms and I couldn't help but wonder what on earth the future held for him.

NINE

Breaking Point

It was going to take time for us all to get used to the new arrangements. Jess now saw her son at the family centre three mornings a week or at a contact centre two afternoons. With the morning sessions, instead of someone coming to pick up Jimmy, I would drop him there myself. It worked well as it meant I could take Lily to school and then go to the family centre with Jimmy on the way back. It also gave me a chance to see Jess and Darren and have a quick chat with them. For the two afternoon sessions, a contact worker would come and collect him from my house and then bring him back to me later on.

Having Jimmy with me full-time enabled me to get into a normal routine. The girls loved having him around and he was a very happy, contented three-month-old who was getting more and more responsive by the day. He had changed so much over the past few weeks. His thick tufty hair was getting a bit lighter and he was looking more and more like Jess every day. He loved lying on his play mat and he kicked his little legs with excitement as he bashed the little animals hanging above his head. He could grip things in his hand now, too, and his favourite toy was a rattle that made a squeaky noise. Every time I pressed it, he'd give me a huge grin.

A few weeks into the new routine it was Christmas. The way it fell this particular year meant that Christmas Day was on a Thursday, Boxing Day was on a Friday and then neither the contact centre nor the family centre would be open until the following Monday, so Jess wasn't going to see her son for four days.

'When can I see Jimmy?' she asked a few days before when she rang. 'Can I come round to your house on Christmas Day?'

'I'm afraid you can't do that, Jess,' I told her. 'All your contact has to be supervised through the centres now, and they're not open over the festive period.'

'But that's too long to go without seeing him,' she said. 'When will I give him his presents?'

'You'll have contact during the day on Christmas Eve, so you'll see him then,' I replied.

'But it's his first Christmas,' she said. 'I can't believe we won't get to spend it with him.'

'Well I'm afraid that's the reality of the choice you've made,' I said. 'I'm not being mean, Jess, those are the rules. You don't live with us any more, so we have to do everything officially now.'

'You're being so unfair,' she said, and I could tell that she was crying. 'Daz is going to be gutted.'

On Christmas Eve Jimmy came back from the contact centre with two presents and a Christmas card.

'Mum and Dad sent those for him,' a worker told me, and I put them under the tree with the rest of the gifts.

I absolutely love Christmas, and it's always a big deal in my house. On Christmas Day the girls were up early as usual to open their stockings. Even though Jimmy was too young to understand, I put him in his bouncy chair so he could watch them and he gazed in wonder at the twinkly lights and sparkling baubles on the Christmas tree. I got Lily to open Jimmy's gifts from Jess and Darren and show them to him. There was a sweet little stuffed dog in one parcel and a selection box in the other.

'Why on earth have they bought him that?' scoffed Louisa. 'He doesn't even eat food yet, so it's a waste of time buying him a load of chocolate.'

'It's the thought that counts,' I told her. 'They want him to know they're thinking of him on Christmas Day.'

They'd also sent him a lovely card.

To our beautiful son on your first Christmas, they'd written. *Sorry we can't be with you. We love you loads and loads. Luv Mummy and Daddy.* The rest of the card was filled with endless rows of kisses.

I knew today must have been hard for them, not being with their baby. That afternoon I took a photo of Jimmy in the little Santa Babygro I'd got him and texted it to Jess.

Merry Christmas Mummy and Daddy love from Jimmy xx, I wrote.

She messaged back straight away.

He looks so cute, she replied. *We're really missing him. I hope he's having a good day.*

Shortly afterwards she rang my mobile.

'How's Jimmy?' she asked. 'Is he having a nice Christmas? We're missing him so, so much.'

'He's having a lovely day,' I said. 'Santa bought him a mobile for his cot and some rattles. He was as good as gold while we had our Christmas dinner and he sat there in the bouncer and nodded off.'

'I can't believe we're not with him,' she sighed. 'It feels like a lifetime until we're going to see him again.'

'How's your day been?' I asked her.

'OK I suppose,' she said. 'They don't make much of a fuss about Christmas at Darren's. They've spent all day getting drunk so me and Daz are just sat in the bedroom.'

'Did you get any nice pressies?' I asked.

'No,' she said. 'But I did get Daz a big packet of baccy and he was really pleased.'

Jess seemed to want to stay on the phone and chat.

'What about the girls?' she asked. 'What did they get?'

'Lily got lots of Sylvanian Family stuff, and Louisa was really chuffed as she got some hair straighteners.'

'I wish I was there with you all,' she said.

'I'm so sorry, sweetie, but I've got to go now,' I told her. 'I promised I'd make everyone turkey sandwiches for tea and Jimmy needs his bath.'

'Give him a big kiss from me,' she said sadly.

'I will do,' I said.

I could tell she was struggling not being with her baby at this time of year.

When New Year came, all the contact sessions went back to normal. However, there was one other surprising development over the festive season that had nothing to do with Jess.

I got a call on the first working day after New Year. When Social Services' number flashed up I assumed it would be Katherine ringing to have a chat about Jess, but to my surprise, it was Lily's social worker, Patricia. She didn't get in touch very often as Lily's contact with her mum had been the same arrangement for years.

'Is everything all right with Lily?' I asked.

'Fine,' she said. 'There's something I need to talk to you about, Maggie. There's been a few developments with Lily's mum, Jane.'

'What's happened?' I asked.

'It seems that Jane has finally split up with Lily's dad. She said she'd had enough and so she's left him.'

'Well, she's left him before and always gone back in the end,' I said.

'This time we think it's for good,' Patricia told me. 'This happened a couple of months ago and she's not gone back to him since. She's got a full-time job so she's financially stable and she's renting her own house now.'

'Good for her,' I said.

To be honest, I was surprised as it was something that I'd never thought would happen.

'Jane got in touch with us a couple of months ago because she wanted to have her contact sessions with Lily at her new house instead of at the contact centre,' she said. 'She also asked if we could look at the possibility of Lily going back to live with her full-time.'

'Gosh,' I gasped, 'that's a quick change of plan. I thought Lily was going to be here permanently.'

After four years of fostering Lily I certainly hadn't been expecting her to move back with her mum.

'Is that not what you think Lily wants?' asked Patricia.

'No, not at all,' I said. 'Lily loves her mum and I think this would be very much what Lily wants. It's just taken me a bit by surprise, if I'm honest.'

Patricia explained that since Jane's request they'd been to see her at her new house and had also done a parenting assessment, which she'd passed with flying colours.

'We've also carried out several spot checks just to make sure Lily's dad isn't living at the house, and there appears to be no sign of him,' she said. 'The house seems fine and suitable for contact, so we thought Lily could start visiting mum there and we'll see how it goes.'

'Why didn't you say anything sooner?' I asked Patricia.

'We wanted to test mum's commitment first,' she said. 'You know how it is. Parents say that's what they want and then lose interest when they have to be assessed, and for all we knew she could have reconciled with dad. But Jane really seems to have started a new life for herself and she wants her daughter back.'

'I'll talk to Lily about contact and let you know,' I said.

When Lily got home from school that night, I had a chat with her.

'Instead of going to see Mummy at the contact centre next week, how would you feel about going to see her at her house?'

Lily's face lit up.

'Yay, will I be able to see my old bedroom?' she asked. 'The one I slept in when I was a little girl?'

'I'm afraid Mummy lives in a different house now to the one she used to live in with Daddy,' I told her. 'I've spoken to your social worker and she said it's a lovely house and to reassure you that Daddy won't be there.'

'I think that would be good,' said Lily. 'I'd like to see it.'

She seemed all excited about going to see her mum in a new place and not the boring contact centre. This was all great news for Lily, but to be honest, it was a huge bombshell for me. After four years, I loved Lily as if she was my own daughter and the thought of potentially having to say goodbye to her was completely devastating.

Meanwhile, as January passed Jimmy seemed to be changing at a rapid pace. He'd lost that scrawny newborn baby look, and every day he seemed to do something new.

One afternoon he was on his play mat when I heard Lily shrieking.

'Maggie, come quick,' she shouted as I came out of the loo.

I ran into the living room thinking something terrible had happened to find Jimmy on his tummy on the carpet with a satisfied look on his face.

'Maggie, he rolled over,' said Lily proudly. 'He did a roly-poly.'

'So he did,' I said. 'You clever boy.'

I went over and ruffled his wispy brown hair and he gave me a big gummy smile. Moments like this were bittersweet. I felt a real sense of joy that he was reaching these milestones – however, it was also tinged with sadness as I thought of Jess and how she should have been here to see this.

I'd bought a special notebook so that when Jimmy went for contact with Jess and Darren, I would write in it and they could read my comments. It was normally very factual stuff like how he'd slept or if he'd been unwell, and Jess and Darren could write things in there for me.

Instead of telling them *Jimmy rolled for the first time*, I wrote, *Jimmy's got something to show you*. Then when he rolled for her and Darren there would still be that element of joy and surprise.

My clever boy rolled over today!!! Jess wrote in the book along with a smiley face.

I'd also put suggestions in the book of things they could do with him during the sessions, so they would still feel like his parents.

There's some baby rice in the nappy bag. As he's coming up to five months, thought you might like to try him on some solids. Have a go and let me know if he takes it.

Jess would send back her reply.

He didn't like that white slop. He blew a raspberry and Daz got it all over him!! I think maybe too soon 4 solids?

I knew she missed Jimmy desperately, especially at the weekends when she wouldn't see him, as she would text me several times each day.

How's J? Is he sleeping OK cos he was teething badly yesterday and grumpy.

I'd try and reassure her.

Don't worry, he's fine, his temp has gone down and he's a lot brighter.

On the days when I dropped Jimmy at the family centre, it would give me a chance to see Jess and Darren and ask how they were getting on. One Monday morning when I walked in with Jimmy, Jess rushed over to us.

'Hello, my little man,' she cooed and Jimmy gave her the biggest smile.

'Look at that grin,' I told her. 'He certainly knows who his mummy is.'

She couldn't wait to get him out of the car seat for a cuddle.

'Oh, I've missed you,' she said, burying her nose in his neck.

'How are you doing?' I asked her.

We were several weeks into the new routine and I noticed that Jess was looking very thin.

'OK,' she said.

'Are you eating properly?' I asked her.

She shrugged. 'Darren's mum's always moaning that she ain't got enough money to feed us all, so we have to make do with what's around or get some crisps or chocolate from the shop if we can afford it,' she said.

'We miss your dinners, Maggie,' Darren told me. 'How are Lily and Louisa?'

'They're fine,' I said. 'Louisa's loving college, and Lily got Monopoly for Christmas so she's obsessed with playing that.'

'Tell Lily next time I see her I'll give her a game and I bet I'll beat her,' he said.

'I will do.' I smiled.

Even though they were both happy to be living together again, I could tell they missed their son and I knew Darren's house was chaotic to say the least. It worried me.

I had a chat to the contact worker and tried to engineer a way for them to have a proper lunch at the family centre.

'Jimmy will be on solids soon, so it's really important for him to see everyone sitting down together as a family and having a meal,' I told her. 'I know that doesn't happen at Darren's house.'

So it was agreed that when they came to the family centre, part of the morning would be spent cooking something together in the kitchen and then, before they left, they'd all sit down for an early lunch. It also meant that Jess and Darren were getting at least one proper meal a day.

For the afternoon sessions, I'd send ham or egg mayo sandwiches and a Tupperware full of cakes with a note.

Jimmy, Louisa and I were baking and we made far too many cakes so we thought you might be able to help us eat them.

I couldn't bear to think of these two youngsters going hungry, and it only proved to me that they needed nurturing and parenting themselves.

Now that Jess was living with Darren, I didn't see Katherine as much, but she would ring me from time to time with updates.

'The first few weeks seem to have gone OK,' she said when she called. 'There's still a lot of shouting and yelling when I see Darren but at least they're turning up to the sessions and the psychological assessment has started.'

The one positive of Jess going to live with Darren was that she seemed stronger somehow now they were together. It was as if being with him had given her her fight back. Their attitude was very 'them and us', so it was she and Darren against Katherine and Social Services. Darren had found them a solicitor and they'd had a meeting with him.

'We told him that Social Services are not having our baby, that he's staying with us,' Jess told me on the phone. 'And we said that what we wanted all along was to be together as a family.'

'Have you heard from the guardian ad litem yet?' I asked Jess.

'The what?' she said. 'What the heck is one of those?'

'Well, you have your solicitor to represent you and Darren, and Social Services have their solicitor. A guardian is somebody who's appointed by the court to represent Jimmy and make sure his needs are being addressed.'

'How can they do that?' she scoffed. 'Jimmy can't talk. He's a baby.'

'His guardian will talk to you and Darren, they'll talk to the health visitor and the contact workers, Katherine and probably me. He or she will probably come to some of your sessions at the family centre and the contact centre too. They'll speak to everyone involved in the case, then they'll make their recommendations to the court about what they think's best for Jimmy.'

'So the guardian is on our side then?' Jess asked.

'There are no sides,' I told her. 'They're representing Jimmy's needs. It's not about whose side people are on. Everyone wants to do what's best for your baby.'

A few days later I spoke to Katherine and she said that a guardian had been appointed. It was a man called Douglas McBride, and Jess told me a few days later that he'd arranged to go and see her and Darren at home.

'What was he like?' I asked Jess when I dropped Jimmy off at the family centre the following week.

'He was really nice,' she said. 'He chatted to us for ages, and him and Daz got on really well and was talking about cars. I think he liked us, and we didn't say nothing wrong.'

'Why wouldn't he like you, Jess?' I asked. 'He's not there to catch you out. I'm glad it went well, and it's good that you felt so relaxed around him.'

A few days later Douglas came round to see me. I could see what Jess had meant. He was a kind-looking man with grey hair and a soft Scottish accent.

He was very natural and relaxed with Jimmy. He picked him up and bounced him up and down on his lap and Jimmy gave him big smiles.

'Well, there's nothing wrong with this wee lad, is there?' He smiled. 'He's a bonny little thing.'

'He is,' I told him. 'He's a very easy baby.'

We talked about Jess and Darren and he asked me about how Jess had been when she'd first come into the placement.

'She was determined to be a good parent,' I said. 'There were a lot of things that she didn't understand or know how to do, but once I'd told her, she got it straight away. She's got a good bond with Jimmy and she's very loving with him.'

I told him how Darren had regularly come round for tea and helped give Jimmy a bath and put him to bed.

'He's a nice lad and I've never had any problems with him,' I said. 'When he and Jess were together with Jimmy here, they looked after the baby well.'

Douglas sat and listened and took notes.

'How did you feel when Jess chose to go and live with Darren rather than stay here with the baby?' he asked.

'I felt very sad,' I said. 'But I know what an incredibly hard decision it was for Jess. She's had a very unstable childhood and she relies on Darren and needs him for her own emotional well-being. I also worry about them being at Darren's, as I know his home life isn't the most stable either.'

'Yes,' agreed Douglas, 'I was only there an hour but there were lots of people coming and going and it all seemed very chaotic. Unfortunately Darren's mother was unwilling to talk to me.'

'Have you chatted to Jess's mum?' I asked.

'She didn't seem to be in any fit state to be able to talk,' he sighed. 'She slammed the door in my face.'

I wasn't surprised, and that would have given him a picture of the kind of childhood that Jess had had.

Douglas didn't give me any indication of what he was thinking, but he seemed very rational and caring and I hoped that he would give Jess and Darren a fair chance.

Maybe things would start turning around for them.

It certainly seemed that way when, a month into the new arrangement, Becky phoned me with good news.

'I heard from Katherine yesterday,' she told me.

'Lucky you,' I sighed.

'Maggie, behave yourself,' she joked. 'For once there appears to have been some good news. The psychologist has finished assessing Jess and Darren and the results seem pretty positive.'

'That's great,' I said.

I was pleased that at long last something had gone in their favour. This report was something that a family court judge would have to take into consideration when they were deciding Jimmy's future.

Becky explained that no evidence had been found of any psychological disturbances or underlying conditions.

'The psychologist commented that Darren sometimes has anger issues with regards to authority figures but that they both had a clear love for their baby,' she said.

I knew the report would give Jess and Darren a boost and it was something positive down on paper for them. Part of me felt sad that they thought everybody was so against them.

Things were going positively for Lily too. She was enjoying going to her mum's house every week, and one night when she was in the bath, she said she had something important to ask me.

'Maggie, do you think I might ever be allowed to go and live with Mummy in her new house?' she asked.

'Would you like to do that?' I said, and she nodded.

'It doesn't mean that I don't like living with you, Maggie, but I haven't lived with Mummy for a very long time and I think she'd like it.'

'I can have a word with your social worker, if you're sure that's what you want?'

'Yes, I do,' she said. 'I definitely do.'

I called Patricia the next day and told her what Lily had said.

'Jane is still very keen for Lily to go back home too,' she told me. 'But she's very much willing to take things slowly and work at Lily's pace.'

Patricia agreed that we would keep the contact going as it was for now and then look to slowly increasing it each month.

However, things weren't working as well with Jess and Darren. One afternoon a worker dropped Jimmy back to me after their afternoon session at the contact centre.

'How did it go today?' I asked her.

I could tell by the look on her face that something had gone on.

'What is it?' I asked. 'What happened?'

'When Jess and Darren came in this afternoon I was sure I could smell alcohol on them,' she said. 'They looked the worse for wear. Their clothes were scruffy and they looked like they hadn't washed.'

'Do you think they were drunk?' I asked, genuinely shocked.

To the best of my knowledge, Jess had never been a drinker or even gone on nights out.

'I don't think so,' she said. 'They seemed more hung-over. I had to mention it to Katherine, though, as they were too tired to do much with the baby and Darren nodded off at one point.'

'What did she say?' I asked, fearing the worst.

'She came and talked to them and they admitted they'd been out the night before and had got back home late and that it must be stale alcohol that I could smell. Darren wasn't very happy with being asked about it,' she said.

'I can imagine,' I sighed.

'Katherine warned them that they had to turn up to contact in a fit state to look after Jimmy, otherwise the session would be cancelled.'

'Hopefully it will be a one-off,' I said. 'Alcohol honestly wasn't an issue when Jess was living with me, and I've never smelt alcohol on either her or Darren.'

The following week I waved Jimmy off with the contact worker who was taking him to the afternoon session. I was puzzled when half an hour later she was back at the front door with him in his car seat.

'What happened?' I asked.

'They didn't turn up,' she said. 'Katherine's been ringing them but neither of them is answering.'

Just when I had thought things were looking up, Darren and Jess were not sticking to the rules and were pushing the boundaries again.

Please don't do this, I thought to myself.

Katherine came round to see me later on.

'Did you get hold of Jess and Darren?' I asked.

'Finally,' she tutted. 'They reckoned they were too poorly to come in but I explained to them that if that's the case, then they need to phone us and let us know.

'As you and I know, when parents don't turn up to contact it's a huge rejection for the child.'

Thankfully Jimmy was too young to realise what was happening but it was very damaging for an older child when their parents didn't turn up.

'I've told them that what's going to happen now is that they have to be at the contact centre half an hour before a session, then we'll ring you and let you know whether Jimmy needs to come in or not.

'If they're a no-show or they're late, then contact will be cancelled, simple as that.'

I was past feeling angry with Jess and Darren. I just had an overwhelming sense of sadness and frustration that they were ruining all their good work again.

That night, Jess phoned me.

'I hope you don't mind me ringing, but I wanted to check how Jimmy was,' she said. 'We didn't get to see him today.'

'So I heard,' I said. 'He's absolutely fine. So what happened? Why didn't you both make it to contact?'

'Oh, I didn't feel very well and some other things was happening,' she said vaguely.

'Jess, it's so, so important that you don't let anything get in the way of seeing your son.'

'Yeah, I know,' she said.

Just like before, things were fine for a few weeks and then they started to slip.

'You've got to keep it up,' I said. 'It's the same old story, but you've got to prove your commitment to Jimmy. If the assessment is stopped, then how can you hope to pass it?'

'It's so exhausting,' she said. 'Every day we've got to be somewhere and it can be really boring. The other day Jimmy fell asleep in the contact worker's car on the way to centre and they wouldn't let me wake him up. We all had to sit there for two hours not doing anything while he had a snooze.'

'It might be boring,' I said. 'Looking after a young baby is sometimes monotonous but if you want your son back then you have to do it,' I told her.

My words had obviously made no difference because the following week Jimmy was returned to me twice – once when the family centre session was cancelled because Jess and Darren had turned up late and another day when they didn't bother turning up at all. Katherine arranged to come round and see me.

'I'm getting increasingly frustrated with the way things are going,' she told me.

'As you know, Darren and Jess were late again earlier this week and then they didn't come the following day.'

'Did they say what happened?' I asked.

'Darren's brother's car apparently broke down so they couldn't get a lift,' she said. 'On the day they didn't turn up, they allegedly had a solicitor's appointment, although they failed to tell anyone that.

'I'm going to have a meeting with my manager to see what she thinks is the best way forward. There's been so much lateness and not turning up, and it's the luck of the draw when they do turn up whether they're willing to engage or not. We can't go on like this.'

The sad thing was, I agreed with her. Jess and Darren weren't giving anyone much choice.

Jess phoned me later that afternoon.

'Has Katherine spoke to you?' she asked me.

'Yep,' I said, 'and I'm not very happy.'

'Maggie, we didn't go to the family centre the other day because we had a solicitor's appointment at 11 a.m.,' she said.

'Yes, but you could still have gone to the centre from 9 a.m. until 10.30 a.m. and had some time with Jimmy beforehand. Why on earth didn't you talk to Social Services, and let them know about the meeting?'

'It was a mistake,' she said. 'I thought Daz had spoken to them and he thought I'd mentioned it.'

'And you were late again the other day,' I told her. 'It's just not good enough.'

'We got there at 9.30 a.m. and Jimmy had already been sent back to you,' she said. 'Darren's brother's car broke down and we had no money for a taxi so we had to get the bus.'

'Jess, it's too late for excuses,' I told her. 'It's always someone else's fault. Everyone's patience is being well and truly tested. As I've told you all along, your actions will have consequences.'

'Yeah, but that psychologist said good things about us,' she said proudly. 'Social Services can't ignore that.'

'Yes, but one report isn't going to convince a judge of your commitment to Jimmy,' I said. 'Everything will be taken into consideration.'

Jess went quiet. I knew I was being hard on her and I was saying things that she didn't want to hear, but unfortunately it was the truth.

I phoned Becky that afternoon and updated her about what had been happening.

'Why do you think they're finding it so hard?' she asked.

'They're kids themselves,' I said. 'Everyone keeps forgetting that they're only sixteen and seventeen, and it's a lot for them to take on board with absolutely no family support. They feel judged, and as if everyone is against them and wants them to fail. They love their baby and they want to be together as a family, but they're struggling.'

'What's the answer then?' said Becky.

'They've been saying all along that they want to be a family,' I said. 'So how about assessing them at a residential centre where all three of them could live together?'

'I have talked about this to Katherine, but I don't think Social Services want to do that partly because of the cost and also because of what they deem to be Darren and Jess's lack of commitment,' said Becky.

I could understand it. Social Services certainly didn't have an endless supply of money, and if they were going to invest in a residential placement they needed to know that Jess and Darren were going to be committed to it.

'I just wish Katherine would give it some more thought and not just dismiss it entirely,' I said. 'She's having a meeting with her manager, so let's see what they decide.'

The following afternoon, my mobile rang.

'Hello,' I said.

No one answered but I could hear someone crying in the background. Huge great gulping sobs.

'Maggie . . .' a voice quivered.

'Jess, lovely?' I said. 'Is that you?'

She was crying so much, she could barely speak.

'Take a deep breath and tell me what's happened,' I said.

'It's Jimmy,' she sobbed.

'What about him?' I asked. 'He's here with me now and he's absolutely fine.'

'Katherine's talked to her manager and they've decided we can't see him no more,' she snivelled. 'She said they're going to stop the family centre assessment and they're going to have a meeting to decide what to do next. I think they're going to get him adopted.'

'Oh, sweetheart,' I said, my heart sinking. 'I don't know anything about this. Whatever has happened, I'm sure they won't just stop you from seeing him. Let me talk to Katherine and find out what's going on and I'll ring you straight back,' I said.

'OK,' she said meekly. 'Thanks.'

I phoned Katherine straight away.

'I've just had a very upset and distressed Jess on the phone,' I said. 'What's going on?'

'I explained to her and Darren that I've spoken to my manager and we've decided that the way things are going at the family centre, there's no point in continuing the assessment. They're not attending enough, they're not committed to being on time and they're not willing to work with us. We can't carry on like that.'

'I know they've found it really hard with all the toing and froing,' I said. 'What about finding them a place in a residential centre so they can be assessed as a family?'

'There's absolutely no point in looking at a residential centre in my opinion,' she said. 'They can't even manage to commit to three hours a few times a week.'

I explained how Jess had told me that they were no longer able to see the baby.

'That's not the case,' said Katherine. 'They'll still have the contact sessions with Jimmy twice a week.'

'Jess was hysterical when she phoned me,' I said. 'Sometimes when she's upset and angry she doesn't really take things in properly, so do you mind if I call her back and explain about the contact?'

'Yes, that's fine,' said Katherine. 'I also explained to her that we're going to hold a case conference as soon as we can. So I'll be in touch about that.'

I called Jess back straight away.

'Yes, they're cancelling the family centre assessment but you'll still have the afternoon contact sessions when you can see Jimmy,' I told her.

'But that's only twice a week,' she said. 'That's nothing.'

'You can request more contact,' I said. 'And we can talk through it at the case conference.'

'What's that?' she asked.

'It's where everyone involved in Jimmy's case meets up – so that will be you, me, Darren, the guardian, the IRO, Katherine and her manager – and then everyone has to say what they think is the best long-term plan for Jimmy and they'll make those recommendations to the court.'

'We've lost him, haven't we?' she said. 'They're going to get him adopted, I know they are.'

'I honestly don't know, Jess,' I told her.

I couldn't reassure her that that wasn't the case because I wasn't sure. I did know that Katherine had been pushing for Jimmy to be adopted since day one.

'They can't take Jimmy away from us,' she sobbed. 'I'll die if they take my baby away. Well, I'm not going to let them.'

TEN

On the Run

Over the next few days I was bombarded with texts from Jess.

I miss my baby.

I can't bear this. It's 2 long til I see him.

Since the family assessment had been cancelled, their last session had been a Thursday and the next contact session wasn't until Tuesday the following week. No matter how unreliable they'd been, I could see Jess was pining for Jimmy and I really felt for her.

'That's five days,' sobbed Jess down the phone. 'I won't see Jimmy for five whole days.'

'Like I said, if you show willing and turn up to contact on time and do everything by the book, then you can ask to have more sessions,' I said.

However, over the next few days I could tell Jess was really struggling. As well as the texts, she rang once a day.

'We're both missing him like mad,' she said. 'It's made us realise what it would be like if he got adopted. I don't think I could cope, Maggie.'

'You're thinking too far in advance,' I told her. 'Nobody knows what's going to happen. You can still prove to Social Services that you can do this.'

I didn't want her just to give up and let it happen.

Instead of a worker picking Jimmy up and taking him to the contact sessions and bringing him back afterwards, I said I'd be happy to do it. It meant I could still see Jess and Darren and keep an eye on how things were going. The night before their contact visit, Jess texted me.

I can't wait to c J tomorrow. Missed him so much.

Later that evening, another text arrived.

Could you send an extra bottle for Jimmy in case he gets hungry?

OK but do you think he's going to need two bottles in two hours? I replied.

He was on solids, so I was trying to reduce his milk intake.

Want to show Katherine that we r organised, she wrote. *U know how he likes his milk.*

OK! I replied.

The following day I set off for the contact centre with Jimmy. I'd packed the nappy bag with an extra bottle for him as Jess had requested. It was a small centre attached to the local Social Services office. As I walked towards reception, I could see Jess and Darren waiting there. When Jess saw me coming in, she ran over to us.

'Jimmy!' she cried. 'Oh, I've missed you so, so much, baby.'

She couldn't get him out of the car seat quick enough. She had tears in her eyes as she cuddled him, stroked his hair and covered him in kisses. Darren was happy to see his son too.

'It's been dead weird not seeing him for this long,' he said. 'Jess has been going out of her mind.'

'Well, you enjoy spending time with him and I'll see you later,' I said.

I'd arranged to pick him at 2.30 p.m., which gave me plenty of time to go and get Lily from school afterwards.

Two hours later I pulled into the car park to collect Jimmy. I could see Jess, Darren and a contact worker called Jane who I knew waiting in reception. When they saw me driving in, they started walking out to the car park to meet me. Darren was carrying Jimmy in the car seat like he normally did when I collected them from the family centre. He would strap him into the back seat of my car before they gave him a kiss goodbye.

As they walked towards us, I could see Jess's eyes were red and her face was puffy.

'Are you OK?' I asked.

'She had a run-in with Katherine,' Darren told me.

'Oh, no,' I sighed. I was conscious that Jane could hear what we were saying so I said: 'You'll have to tell me about it later.'

As we walked across the car park to where I'd parked, out of the corner of my eye I noticed a blue car reversing out of a space nearby.

Jess suddenly turned to me. Her face had drained of all colour and she was shaking.

'What is it, Jess?' I asked. 'Are you OK?'

'I'm so sorry, Maggie,' she whispered. 'This is the only way.'

'What?' I said, puzzled. 'What on earth are you talking about?'

'We just want to be with Jimmy,' she said. 'He's our baby and no one's taking him away from us. That's why we're doing this.'

'Doing what?' I asked, really confused now.

There was no time for her to answer. Everything that happened next took place so quickly, I felt powerless to stop it. The blue car that had reversed out of the parking space suddenly pulled up to a halt beside us.

'Get in!' Darren yelled to Jess.

She opened the passenger door and jumped into the front seat.

'Darren, what the hell are you doing?' I shouted as he opened the door, pushed Jimmy into the back seat and jumped in next to him. Before I had time to do anything, he slammed the door and the car screeched off.

'Jess!' I yelled, running after them. 'Darren! Please don't do this. This is madness. It isn't going to solve anything.'

But it was too late. All I could do was watch in horror as the car sped out of the car park and drove off down the road.

I stood there, stunned. My heart was thumping out of my chest, my head was spinning. What the heck had just happened?

'I'd better get the social worker,' said Jane, dashing back into the building.

A few seconds later Katherine came running out, her face red with rage.

'What happened?' she said. 'Where have they gone?'

'They've taken the baby,' I said. 'They've snatched Jimmy.'

'What?' she gasped. 'How could they take a baby from right in front of you?

'Why on earth didn't you do something or try and stop them, Maggie?'

I couldn't believe she was blaming me.

'It all happened in a matter of seconds,' I said. 'I wasn't going to try and grab the baby off Darren. It wouldn't be safe near a moving car.'

'Well, who was driving?' she asked. 'Did you get the registration number? You must have seen something, for God's sake.'

'Katherine, I told you, it all happened so fast,' I said. 'It came completely out of the blue.'

I'm useless with cars at the best of times, and I'm one of those people that doesn't know the difference between a Porsche and a Punto.

'I'm sorry I didn't get the number plate,' I told her. 'All I know is that it was a small blue car. There wasn't time to even see who was driving it. I think it was a man.'

Katherine shook her head. 'This has gone too far now,' she sighed. 'How could they do something so stupid? I'm fed up with their silly games.'

A few minutes later her manager, Martin, came out.

'Maggie, I've just heard what happened,' he said. 'Are you OK?'

It was only then that I realised my whole body was shaking.

'I think I'm a bit shocked,' I said.

'Come inside and sit down and we'll get you a cup of tea,' he said.

It was nice to be shown a little bit of kindness rather than the interrogation Katherine was subjecting me to. Martin took me into his office and sat with me. After a couple of sips of tea, I felt a lot calmer.

'I can't believe they've done this,' I said. 'I honestly had no inkling that this was going to happen. I know Jess has been upset about the family centre assessment being cancelled and only seeing Jimmy twice a week, but never in a million years did I think she and Darren would do something like this.'

'Maggie, it's not your fault,' he said. 'There's nothing you could have done to stop them. It would have been too risky if you'd tried to grab the car seat off Darren. You can't be grappling with a young baby near a moving car. You did the right thing. Katherine's calling the police now to report it.'

I looked at the clock and suddenly realised the time.

'Oh no,' I said, 'I'm supposed to be doing the school run. Lily will wonder where I am.'

I got my mobile out and phoned my friend Vicky who was also a foster carer and had children at the same school.

'Hi, Vic, there's been a bit of an emergency at the contact centre and I wondered if you could pick Lily up from school for me?'

'Of course,' she said. 'Are you OK, Maggie? What's happened? You sound dreadful.'

'It's a long story but Jess and Darren have absconded with Jimmy,' I said.

'What?' she gasped. 'Oh no. Listen, I've got your spare key so I'll take Lily back to your house and see you there later.'

'Thank you,' I said. 'I don't know how long I'm going to be here as the police will need to speak to me.'

When I put the phone down, Katherine was back.

'The police are on their way,' she said.

'Have you got any idea, Maggie, who might have been driving or where they might have gone?' Martin asked me.

I shrugged. I felt so helpless.

'I didn't really see who was driving but I think it was a man,' I said. 'All I saw was the back of his head as they drove off.'

'I bet it was one of Darren's brothers,' said Katherine. 'They've all got records as long as your arm.'

I ignored her.

'As for where they might have gone, all I can think of is Darren's house,' I said.

'The police are already checking that address to see if they're there and I've given them Jess's mum's details,' added Katherine. 'That's all we have on file.'

Katherine was still reeling after what had happened and was obviously looking for someone to blame.

'What I can't get my head round is why you let them go, Maggie. Why did you let them take the baby from right in front of you?'

I was losing patience with her now.

'Katherine, for months I've been bringing Jimmy to this family centre and collecting him,' I told her. 'Darren and Jess have come out with the baby and met me in the car park and there's never, ever been a problem. I didn't know this was going to happen. It was as much a shock to me as it was to you, and blaming me isn't going to change what happened or help bring them back.'

I could sense Martin had had enough too.

'It's OK, Katherine, I think I can handle this from now on,' he told her. 'I'll sit with Maggie. Why don't you go and get yourself a cup of tea?'

'OK,' she huffed, obviously not happy about the fact that she was being sent out of his office.

'I'm sorry about the overzealous questioning, Maggie,' Martin said to me when she'd left. 'Katherine's taken this very hard. Of course we don't think you could have done anything to stop what happened today.'

'Good,' I said. 'Jimmy's safety is paramount. I just hope you find them quickly.'

'Was Jess particularly upset about anything?' he asked.

'When she came out of the contact centre she looked like she'd been crying, and Darren said to me that she and Katherine had had a run-in,' I told him.

'A run-in?' he questioned. 'What do you mean?'

Things had gone too far now, and I couldn't keep quiet any more.

'I think you've got to look at the relationship between Jess, Darren and Katherine,' I said. 'She's always been so hostile to them right from the beginning.

'I don't think either of them ever felt they had a chance of keeping Jimmy with her as their social worker.

'I know they haven't been consistent, and I know they're constantly pushing the boundaries, but the way she deals with them just makes them fly off the handle.

'Having her as their social worker is not working, and this needs to work, for Jimmy. They need to feel like they're being given a fair chance.'

Martin seemed to have taken my opinion seriously, but after everything that had happened today, I feared it might be too late.

'I'm sorry to hear that you feel so strongly,' he said. 'Obviously I need to deal with this situation first, but when this is all over I'd like to have a chat to you in a bit more detail about what's been going on.'

'Thank you,' I said. 'I'd appreciate that.'

Another social worker popped her head round the office door.

'We're just on the phone to the police,' she said. 'Maggie, could you tell me what Jimmy was wearing today?'

I wracked my brains.

'Er, he had on denim dungarees and a stripy T-shirt,' I said.

I finished my cup of tea and Martin went out to see what was happening. Twenty minutes later he came back to see me.

'The police have got initial descriptions of the three of them and they're sending officers round to Darren's house and Jess's mum's place, so I think that's all we can do for now,' he said.

'They're going to want to talk to you, but I appreciate that you've got your other foster children to think about. So why don't you go home, keep your phone on and the police will come round and speak to you there.'

'That would be great,' I said. 'Thank you.'

When I got back, Vicky was there and all the kids were happily playing. Louisa was going to a friend's after college, so she wasn't around. There was a pan of pasta bubbling away on the hob.

'I wasn't sure how long you'd be so I started tea for the kids,' she said.

'Thanks so much,' I said. 'I'm glad to be home.'

'How are you?' she asked.

I shrugged. 'Still a little bit shaken up,' I said.

'What on earth were they thinking?' asked Vicky.

'I've no idea,' I sighed. 'I know they were terrified about the prospect of Jimmy being taken off them and they were upset because they hadn't seen him for five days, but this has really blown their chances now. I just hope they find them sooner rather than later.'

Fifteen minutes later, the doorbell rang.

'That will probably be the police,' I said to Vicky. 'Do you mind keeping an eye on Lily?'

'I'll give them tea in the kitchen so you can chat to them in private in the front room,' she said.

I let the officers in. There were two of them – a man and a woman. I made them a cup of tea and took them through to the living room.

'Can you talk us through what happened when you got to the contact centre earlier?' the male officer asked. 'Did you see anything suspicious when you arrived?'

'Not at all,' I said. 'Jess looked a bit upset, so I went over to her and asked if she was OK and Darren said she'd had a bit of a telling-off from the social worker.

'Then she said she was sorry for what she was about to do and the pair of them jumped in the car with Jimmy.

'It came completely out of the blue,' I told them. 'I was so shocked. We've done this handover so many times before and there's never been an issue. Neither of them is considered a security risk.'

Some contact sessions were held at the larger Social Services buildings where there are security guards and panic buttons. Children are dropped off at reception and taken into the sessions by a designated worker and not the foster carer.

'It all happened within a matter of seconds,' I said. 'The car pulled up, they both jumped in it and put the baby seat on the back seat and screeched off. Honestly, there was nothing I could have done to stop it.'

They asked me again what Jimmy had been wearing and what was in the change bag they'd taken with them.

'Just the usual things,' I said. 'A bottle of milk. No, there were two bottles today, actually, as I'd put in an extra one.'

'Why was that?' asked the female officer.

'Jess texted me last night and asked me to put two in today.'

Suddenly the penny dropped.

'So you think this was all pre-planned?' I asked.

'It seems that way,' she said. 'The contact worker told us that during today's sessions Darren went out for ten minutes to make an urgent phone call, so we think that this was all organised well in advance and wasn't a spur-of-the-moment thing. They'd obviously arranged for the car to be there at the right time.'

'What else was in the bag?' asked the male officer, taking notes.

'A pack of wipes, seven or eight nappies . . .'

'Do you usually send in that many?' he asked.

'It's a change bag that I use as well as the parents, so I always keep it well stocked,' I said. 'I always put plenty in, just in case.'

I also described how there was a change of clothes in there and a little coat.

'A coat?' the officer asked. 'But he wasn't going out anywhere, and you were in the car.'

'I always keep one in there just in case he gets chilly and we're out and about,' I said. 'Even though it's March, it can still feel cold from time to time.'

With all the questions it was hard for me not to feel under suspicion. But I knew they were only doing their job, and they had to check whether I had colluded with Jess and Darren and helped them to arrange this.

'Do you think we should be concerned about the baby's well-being?' he asked. 'Do you think the parents are capable of hurting the baby?'

I shook my head.

'I'm confident that they would never hurt Jimmy,' I said. 'Jess is a good mum.

'They're two scared teenagers who love their baby but who are also very frustrated with the way things are going.

'In their heads they're probably not doing anything wrong. Jimmy is their flesh and blood, so they're taking back what's rightfully theirs. They're terrified that he's going to be taken off them, and fear sometimes makes us do silly things.'

The female officer shook her head.

'I can't imagine it,' she said. 'My little girl's nine months old. I can't imagine how desperate I'd feel if someone was trying to take her off me.'

'Desperate is exactly what they are,' I said.

The officers explained that they'd been to Darren's house but there was no sign of them there and no one knew where they were. There had been no answer at Jess's mum's flat.

'We'll keep on trying,' the officer told me. 'We've called their mobiles but they're going straight to voicemail.

'Obviously if either of them get in contact with you then please let us know.'

'Of course,' I said.

'Where do you think they might have gone?' the woman officer asked.

'I don't think they'll be far away,' I said. 'They don't have any money or family support. Neither they nor the baby have passports, so thankfully I don't think they'll try and leave the country.

'All they have is each other and Jimmy,' I said. 'I suspect they won't have thought this through properly and they'll be running scared. Now they've actually got Jimmy they won't know what to do or where to turn.'

I also mentioned the night Jess hadn't turned up and the police had found her and Jimmy at Darren's friend's house.

'I'll go through my recordings and get you the incident number so you can look up the friend's name and address,' I said.

Half an hour later the police left. All I could do was carry on as normal and keep checking my phone for news. After tea, Vicky took her kids home.

'Keep in touch and let me know if there's any news,' she said.

'I will do,' I told her.

I tried to keep busy; I tidied up then ran Lily a bath.

'Where's baby Jimmy?' she asked when I was reading her a story.

'Oh, he's with his mummy and daddy at the minute,' I said, relieved I was actually able to tell the truth.

I'd put Lily to bed when my mobile rang, and I pounced on it.

'Oh, Becky,' I said. 'I thought it was the police.'

'I'm so sorry, Maggie, I've been in training all day today and I've just seen an email from Katherine about what happened.

'Are you OK?' she asked.

'I'm fine,' I said. 'But there's still no sign of Jess, Darren or the baby.'

'This isn't going to look good for them,' she said.

'I know,' I sighed. 'But I don't think they've done this out of malice. I think it was out of pure fear of losing their baby.'

I told Becky how I'd mentioned something to Katherine's manager about her attitude.

'I said I thought her relationship with them was more harmful than productive and that Jess and Darren need to have someone they can work with. She's always had too much bias against their families to give them both a fair chance.'

'Were you this blunt with him?' Becky laughed.

'No,' I said. 'But I told him in no uncertain terms that when Jimmy comes back and this is all over it's something that needs to be looked at.'

'I completely agree,' said Becky.

'You sound tired, Maggie,' she added. 'You really should try and get some sleep after the day you've had.'

'I will,' I said. 'I'm just going to update my notes and then I'll get my head down.'

After an hour in front of the computer I tried to sleep but I couldn't. I was consumed by fear and worry, but not for Jimmy. I knew in my heart that Darren and Jess loved their son and that they would look after him. My concerns were for them, and the repercussions this whole incident was going to have on their case. They'd dug themselves a great big hole and I had no idea how they were going to get out of it. All I could do was pray that they would see sense and either come back or take Jimmy to the nearest police station and hand themselves in. They had to, because the longer this went on, the worse it would be in the end.

ELEVEN

Repercussions

Despite thinking there was no way I'd ever be able to sleep, I must have nodded off eventually. That was until I was disturbed by my mobile ringing.

Disorientated, I sat bolt upright in bed and looked at my clock. It read 1.30 a.m. I grabbed my phone off the bedside table. Blinking in the harsh glow of the screen, I squinted down at the number flashing up.

It was Jess.

Panicked that I would miss her call, I quickly answered it before it went to voicemail.

'Jess,' I gasped. 'Where are you?'

'I can't tell you,' she whispered. She was talking so quietly I could hardly hear her, and I could tell that she was crying.

'Are you safe?' I asked gently. 'Is Jimmy safe?'

'What do you mean?' she snivelled.

'I need to know that you're not walking the streets and that you, Jimmy and Darren are somewhere safe and warm.'

'Yeah,' she said. 'We're all OK. Jimmy's fine, he's asleep.

'I'm so sorry, Maggie,' she said. 'We didn't think it through and now I don't know what to do. I'm really scared.'

Jess was sobbing now.

'Calm down,' I told her, my head spinning with a mixture of relief, sadness and frustration. 'It's OK.'

'We're in big trouble, aren't we? Katherine's definitely going to take Jimmy away from us now, ain't she?'

'It's not up to Katherine,' I said. 'What I do know is the longer you're away with Jimmy, the worse it's going to be.

'The best thing you can do is hand yourselves in,' I urged her. 'Take Jimmy back to Social Services.'

'No way,' she said. 'We ain't talking to Katherine or Social Services.'

'Well, come here,' I told her. 'Bring Jimmy back to my house and we can talk.'

'I don't want you to get into trouble,' she said. 'And I don't want to bring Jimmy back to no one. We want to keep him.'

'What about the police?' I suggested. 'Would you at least talk to them? They're nothing to do with Social Services. You can tell them how you're feeling and what you're worried about.'

'What's the point?' she sighed. 'You've all got it in for us.'

'That's not true, Jess,' I said. 'Everyone has been worried sick about all three of you.

'Please tell me where you are,' I begged.

'I can't,' she said. 'Daz would go mad. He's asleep at the minute. He don't even know I'm calling you.'

'If you won't tell me where you are, then please tell the police,' I said. 'Jess, you need to understand that I have to tell them that you've phoned me.

'So why don't I get them to call you straight back on your mobile and you can have a chat to them? No obligations. You don't have to tell them where you are if you don't want to. Just talk to them.'

'I don't know,' she sobbed. 'I don't know what to do any more to get us out of this mess.'

'You've got to hand yourselves in,' I said. 'This can't go on any longer. You need to bring Jimmy back.'

'I know,' she said. 'But I'm scared about what's going to happen to us.'

'So please talk to the police,' I told her. 'It will come up as an unknown number, so make sure you leave your phone on and answer it. Promise me that you'll talk to them, Jess?'

There was no answer. She'd hung up.

I was relieved that Jess had got in touch and that they were safe and not sleeping rough, but I was still worried about them. She'd sounded so upset and scared.

I turned the light on and rang the officers who were dealing with the case.

'I've just had a call from Jess,' I told an officer. 'She wouldn't tell me where she was, but if you ring her back now, hopefully she will talk to you and you can convince her to hand herself in.'

'Did she mention the baby?' he asked.

'She said Jimmy was fine and fast asleep, and I've got no reason not to believe her.'

'OK,' he said. 'We'll give her a call now.'

'Would you mind ringing me back when you've spoken to her?' I asked. 'Just to put my mind at rest.'

Whatever happened, I knew there was no chance of me getting any more sleep now. I got up and made myself a cup of tea, my mobile next to me. It was another half an hour before the officer phoned back.

'Well?' I asked. 'What did she say? Did you manage to persuade her?'

'We tried ringing her mobile but there was no answer, I'm afraid,' he told me. 'I tried five or six times and now it's turned off.'

I was disappointed and frustrated.

'How did she sound when you spoke to her?' he asked me.

'Scared, desperate, worried,' I said. 'They're two vulnerable kids who don't have a clue what they're doing, and it's slowly hitting them that they're in a lot of trouble.'

'We've still got a few leads to follow up, so we'll keep you posted,' he said.

All I could hope was that Jess had taken what I'd said on board and would convince Darren that the best thing to do was hand themselves in.

My mind was whirring as I put the kettle back on and made another cuppa. I debated whether to try and ring Jess myself or text her, but I knew I had to be really careful. I was employed by Social Services to be Jimmy's carer. Everything I did had to be in his best interests and I couldn't look like I was colluding with Jess and Darren. I tried to keep busy to take my mind off things. By the time the sun came up on that crisp spring morning, I'd already cleaned the kitchen and I was halfway through a pile of ironing.

'Is Jimmy coming back today?' Lily asked as she tucked into her porridge. 'I miss him.'

'I don't know, love,' I said.

Louisa looked puzzled. She'd come back late from her friend's house so she hadn't noticed he wasn't there until now.

'Where's he gone?' she asked.

This was confidential information that didn't affect her directly, so I wasn't able to tell her what was going on.

'He's with his mummy and daddy,' Lily piped up.

Louisa looked at me quizzically.

'Oh, is he going back to live with Jess and Darren now?' she said.

'That's who he's with at the moment,' I told her. 'But you know how quickly plans change.'

When the girls had left for school and college, I phoned Becky to update her.

'Jess rang me last night,' I told her, and I explained what had happened.

'You've done everything you can,' she said. 'How are you feeling about it all today?'

'I'm sick with worry,' I said. 'I could hear how desperate and scared Jess was on the phone. I want them to do the right thing and hand themselves in but I don't know if that will happen.'

'What are you going to do today?' she asked.

'There's not a lot I can do except keep my mobile with me and stay at home just in case they turn up here.'

The morning dragged. I threw myself into more cleaning but there was no news. At lunchtime I called the police.

'I'm afraid there are no updates,' an officer told me.

They'd been round to Darren's friend's house who they had been staying with before but he hadn't seen them. Darren's brothers and his mum were saying they had no knowledge of what had gone on, nor had they heard from them, and Jess's mum was still AWOL.

'Can you think of anywhere else they might be?' the officer asked.

'Honestly, I'm at a loss,' I said. 'I can't think of anyone else you can try.'

I knew how scared they were, and if they weren't thinking rationally my main fear was that they'd do something stupid.

Please let Jimmy be safe, I thought.

Just after 3 p.m. the doorbell rang. I assumed it was Louisa back from college.

'Have you forgotten your key again, young lady?' I scolded as I opened the door.

'Oh,' I said, surprised to see a police officer stood there.

Then I saw the car seat next to him on the step.

'Jimmy!' I cried. 'Thank God you're back.'

I bent down and stroked his rosy little cheek and he gave me a big smile. Thankfully he looked perfectly happy and healthy.

'What happened?' I asked the officer as I carried the car seat inside. 'Where did you find them?'

'We didn't,' he said. 'They handed themselves in about an hour ago at the police station in town.'

It was such a relief to have Jimmy back and know they were all safe.

'The baby seems fine,' the officer said. 'The police doctor looked him over and he decided there wasn't any need for a hospital check-up.

'Obviously keep an eye on him, and if you have any concerns then seek medical advice straight away.'

'He looks content enough to me,' I said as I lifted him out of the car seat and gave him a cuddle. It was such a relief feeling the weight of his warm little body back in my arms. As he nestled his head into my neck, I breathed in his lovely sweet baby smell and I realised how much I'd grown to care for him.

'How are Jess and Darren?' I asked.

'Very upset,' he told me. 'Especially mum. My colleagues are chatting to them now, and their social worker is on her way over to talk to them.'

Katherine, I thought. Just what they needed. I hoped she'd go easy on them.

'At least they did the right thing in the end and came back,' I said. 'Do you know where they've been?'

He shook his head.

'No idea, but I'm sure they'll tell my colleagues. We wanted to get the baby back to you as soon as we could.'

When the officer left, I warmed up a bottle for Jimmy. He can't have been hungry as he didn't seem interested in either milk or finger food. He'd come back with the changing bag, which was practically empty now. He was wearing a new pair of jeans and a jumper that I didn't recognise and his nappy was dry and had recently been changed.

'I was right,' I said. 'Your mummy and daddy looked after you well, didn't they, little man?'

It was almost as if he understood what I'd said as he babbled something and gave me a huge smile.

I decided to give him a bath as I suspected they probably hadn't had the chance to do that. It would also be an opportunity to check him over myself.

Afterwards I called Becky back to tell her Jimmy had been returned.

'I've given him a bath and he seems absolutely fine,' I said. 'There're no marks or bruises on him. He's clean and well fed and isn't upset or distressed.'

'What a relief,' she said. 'Where are Jess and Darren now?'

'At the police station, but Social Services are on their way over. Katherine's probably about to read them the riot act.'

I didn't have to wait very long to find out what was going on. My phone beeped as a text arrived from Jess.

R u cross with me?

All that matters is you did the right thing in the end, I replied.

How is J? she asked.

He's fine. You looked after him well. How are you feeling?

Tired, she wrote. *Still with police. Waiting for Social Services to give us a telling-off.*

I was also waiting for Katherine to get in touch with me as I knew she'd want to come round to see Jimmy. However, it was her manager Martin who phoned me an hour later.

'Thank goodness they're all back,' he said. 'Would you mind if I came round to check on the baby and have a chat?'

'Not at all,' I said.

He seemed a very measured, calm man, and that was much more preferable than having Katherine coming round and flying off the handle.

'How's Jimmy doing after his ordeal?' he asked when he arrived.

'Oh, he's absolutely fine,' I told him. 'He seems completely unscathed, as you can see.'

He was sitting in his high chair banging some plastic stacking cups together.

'As I suspected, he's been well looked after by his parents,' I said. 'How are Jess and Darren doing?'

'We've spoken to them and they're full of remorse about what they've done,' he said.

'Did they say where they'd been?' I asked.

'Oh, at a friend of Jess's about an hour away. It wasn't a very well-thought-out plan. They didn't have much cash with them, and I think the enormity of what they'd done suddenly hit them and they both panicked.'

'The main thing is the baby's fine,' I said. 'What's going to happen to them now?'

'We've agreed that we don't think there's any point in the police pressing criminal charges,' he said. 'We've always treated this as a missing persons inquiry, not a child abduction, and I don't think there's anything to be gained from putting Jess and Darren through the legal system. That's not going to help anyone, especially Jimmy.'

It was a huge relief to hear that.

'I completely agree,' I said. 'All three of them are vulnerable.'

'However, they do need to know that their actions have consequences,' he said. 'They can't just go taking their child like that without permission.

'A record of what has happened will go on their file which could eventually go towards a court hearing and potentially strengthen the argument for adoption,' he said.

'The more immediate consequences are that any contact Jess and Darren now have with Jimmy will have to be held at a secure contact centre in town.'

'Will I still be able to take him?' I asked.

Martin nodded.

'You can drop him off and collect him, but from now on you'll be handing him to a member of staff who will take him into the contact room rather than handing him directly over to the parents.'

'So I won't be able to see Jess or Darren at contact?'

Martin shook his head.

I felt sad about that. I liked seeing them and hearing about how they were doing and what was going on. I knew they both trusted me and valued my advice.

'How much contact will they be allowed?' I asked.

'Two mornings a week at first,' he said. 'If things go well then we might look at increasing it, but you know as well as I do how hard it is getting an available slot as that centre is extremely busy.'

'If you can't get a space at the centre, perhaps you could look at doing an additional couple of times a week here?' I suggested. 'Jess and Darren could come round for two hours in the early evening and I would be here at all times to supervise them.'

'I think you're jumping the gun a bit, Maggie,' he said. 'That's a long way off in the future at this point. Jess and Darren have got a lot of proving themselves to do first.

'They need to understand that taking Jimmy like that without permission wasn't exactly exemplary behaviour, and we need to build the trust back up between us all again. They need to show that they're willing to work with us.'

While I agreed that taking the baby had been an impetuous and extremely silly move, I didn't think he was seeing the full picture.

'I'm sure you'll agree that this is all about Jimmy's needs,' I said. 'And no matter what happened, Jimmy's needs were met by his parents.

'Despite all the upset and drama, the baby didn't come back starving or bruised or hurt or upset. He had clean clothes and a clean nappy on. There wasn't a mark on him, and he was happy and smiling.

'The only thing that had changed was that he slept in a different place, which I think you'll agree isn't going to cause any long-term damage.'

'I can see what you're saying,' said Martin. 'But they need to understand that what they did wasn't right. Jess and Darren have to prove their commitment and start building up trust again if they want to see Jimmy.'

'Then I honestly think you have to find a new person to work with them who can help them do that, because I can assure you there's no way that's going to happen with their current social worker,' I told him.

'Maggie, I took your concerns about Katherine on board, and her perhaps not being the right person for this case. I can assure you that the issue is under discussion but no decisions have been made yet,' he told me.

'Thank you,' I said. 'I appreciate that.'

Before he left I checked with him if it was still OK for me to speak to Jess.

'Does she ring much?' he asked.

'Not so much as it's expensive,' I said. 'But on the days she doesn't see Jimmy she likes to text.'

'That's fine,' he said. 'Can you just keep it to texting then, please, as it means we've got a record of it in case we need to use it in court.'

'Of course,' I said.

A couple of days later I got a phone call from Becky.

'What have you been saying to Martin?' she said. 'You've

certainly thrown the cat among the pigeons at Social Services.'

'Why?' I laughed.

'I had a phone call from him today in which he described you as a very insightful woman, and said that your concerns about Katherine were valid and had been backed up by other individuals.'

'And?' I asked.

'And she's been taken off this case,' she said. 'Jess will be getting a new social worker assigned to her ASAP.'

My initial reaction was to yell 'Yes!' and punch the air with jubilation, but I knew that wasn't very professional.

'I'm sure Katherine's heart was in the right place, but the way she went about things, and the way she treated Jess and Darren, meant nothing was ever going to go in their favour,' I said.

At least now with a new social worker they might stand a fighting chance of keeping Jimmy.

Katherine hadn't done anything wrong; in fact, she'd followed procedure by the book. But she had failed to build a relationship with these two young parents. It had been hard work for me dealing with her, never mind them. No matter what had gone on previously in their families with Social Services, they couldn't be held accountable and judged for that. Their families' pasts didn't necessarily mean they couldn't be good parents themselves.

Good news spreads fast, and soon I got a text from Jess.

Guess wat? We have a new social worker. No more Katherine!! The police made Social Services listen.

I smiled to myself.

How do u feel about that? I wrote.

V happy, she replied.

Please don't think that by running off with Jimmy you have got your own way, I said.

I know that. We r v sorry and promise we won't do it again.

★

In a strange way, Jess and Darren snatching Jimmy had brought things to a head and led to some positive changes. But it was important that they didn't think they were being rewarded for doing something so reckless. I knew that when the new contact started they would understand the reality of what they'd done. The secure centre had a series of very bare, basic rooms with a box of toys in the corner. There was no kitchen or bedroom and they were very limited as to what they could do there. They couldn't make Jimmy his food or sit down for lunch together or let him have a nap. It was a lot more stark and sterile, and there were panic buttons and security guards constantly on duty.

They might have handed themselves in and Jimmy, thankfully, was fine, but they needed to know that silly, impetuous teenage behaviour wasn't going to work. It was time to knuckle down and show their commitment to Social Services. Because this time, there would be no more chances.

TWELVE

Decision Time

Within a week of Katherine being taken off the case, a new social worker was appointed. Her name was Debbie and she came round to see me a few days later.

As far as first impressions go, I got a bit of a surprise when I opened the door to her. With her heavy make-up, manicured nails and towering high heels, she was much more glamorous than any social worker I'd ever dealt with. She seemed very warm and friendly and was on the ball. She'd clearly read the case file and knew everything that had been going on with Jess and Darren.

'So, Maggie, how did *you* get on with Katherine?' she asked me.

I gave her the diplomatic answer.

'As a foster carer, you don't always see eye to eye with everybody but you learn to get on with them as it's in the child's best interests,' I said, before adding my concerns that she had preconceived ideas of Jess and Darren based on their families' pasts.

'Well, I'm determined this is going to be a fresh start.' She smiled. 'Now, tell me about Jess . . .'

She asked me to tell her what Jess had been like when she first came to the placement, what her relationship was like with Jimmy and how he reacted when he was with her. I described too how, in the early days, Darren had come round for meals and had helped put Jimmy to bed.

'Did that work well, and is that something you'd possibly like to try again?' she asked.

'Yes, it did,' I said. 'My other kids grew very fond of Jess and Darren, and I think doing something like that promotes a sense of family. As Jimmy gets older and more aware, that's very important for him.'

Debbie talked me through the new contact set-up.

'I think they're going to find it difficult so it will be a good test for them,' she said. 'It's a much more sterile environment and they won't have as much freedom. However, if they co-operate with us and it's going well, then after four weeks we will relook at the situation and perhaps increase the amount of contact or find different ways of doing it.

'I'm sure you'll appreciate that we've had to take this measure in response to what happened recently,' she said.

I nodded. 'I'm not trying to excuse what they did, but when they went off with Jimmy they weren't thinking straight,' I told her. 'They were terrified that he was going to be taken away from them.'

'I understand that when people are motivated by panic and fear they sometimes act in an irrational manner,' she replied. 'This is a last chance to prove themselves, so let's see how they get on.'

I was really impressed by Debbie. She seemed compassionate and willing to listen. When Jimmy woke up from his sleep, she took the time to stay and play with him.

'He seems very happy and content,' she said.

'Oh, he is,' I told her.

'Does he have a strong bond with Jess?' she asked.

'Definitely,' I said. 'He knows who his mummy is.'

I showed her the photographs that I'd attached to the skirting boards in the living room so that they were at Jimmy's level. I'd printed out photos of all the people in the house as well as Jess and Darren, and when Jimmy was playing I'd show him the photos of Mummy and Daddy and we'd blow them a kiss goodnight and play peekaboo with them.

'It's something I like to do with all babies and children from Jimmy's age and older who still see their birth parents,' I said.

'You probably think I'm mad doing that with a six-month-old, but I think it's important to include his parents in his daily routine. It means that although Jimmy might not see Jess and Darren every day, they're still familiar to him.'

'I think it's a lovely idea,' she said. 'You and I will keep in touch, and fingers crossed this new contact is a fresh start for everyone,' she added, while gathering her things to leave. She'd stayed for a couple of hours, and I felt a renewed sense of hope that things might take a turn for the better.

Jess, however, didn't seem as enamoured with Debbie as I was.

She's better than Katherine, she wrote. *But Daz says we have to be dead careful as she's still a social worker.*

You need to try and trust her, I texted back. *It's important to have a good relationship with your social worker and have them on side.*

A few days later it was time for me to take Jimmy to the new contact centre to see Jess and Darren. It was a huge 1960s office block in the centre of town with two security guards flanking the revolving doors at the entrance. It was always intimidating for me coming somewhere like this, so God knows how Jess and Darren were going to feel. I carried Jimmy in in his car seat and joined the long queue for reception. There were five people on the desk and they all sat behind a Perspex screen with a grate that you had to talk through.

'Can you sign in, please?' asked the sulky-faced receptionist. 'I've buzzed up and somebody will be down to meet you.'

The new contact worker came down to see me and to introduce herself. She was a woman in her fifties called Lesley and she seemed very chatty and nice.

'Have Jess and Darren arrived yet?' I asked as we walked towards the lifts.

'Yes, Mum and Dad are here and very excited about seeing the baby,' she said. 'Poor Dad's full of cold and looks a bit under the weather, but he said he was determined to come.'

I was relieved that they were there and had both made it on time.

'I'm afraid you're not allowed to go past this point, so I'll take the baby from here,' she told me.

'No problem,' I said, handing her the car seat. 'I'll be back for him in a couple of hours.'

I watched while she disappeared off into the lift, saying a silent prayer under my breath that things were going to go well.

When I went back to pick him up, Jimmy was already waiting in reception with Lesley. He seemed very happy and content and kicked his legs with glee when I bent down and said hello to him in the car seat.

'He's had a lovely time,' she said. 'Mum was on the floor playing with him for ages and they were both very excited to see that he's almost sitting up on his own now.'

'That's brilliant.' I smiled, sighing with relief. 'I'm so glad it went well.'

Later that night, Jess sent me a text message.

Contact went ok I think, she wrote. *Room wasn't very nice and the toys were mucky. Didn't like J putting them in his mouth.*

Do you want me to send some toys in with him from here? I suggested.

Yes please xxx

I was relieved that things seemed to have got off to a good start. It was also handy to have someone like Lesley as a contact worker who was a bit gossipy and would tell me a little bit more than she needed to.

I needn't have worried. As the first few weeks went by, all the signs were good. Jess and Darren turned up on time, they didn't miss a single session and by all accounts were attentive, playing with Jimmy, reading to him and interacting with him.

Three weeks in, Debbie phoned me one afternoon.

'Can I pop round and see you today, Maggie?' she asked. 'There are a couple of things I want to chat to you about.'

'Of course,' I said.

I was feeling hopeful for good news. The first month of the new contact arrangement was coming to an end and I was hoping Social Services were going to look into giving Jess and Darren more time with Jimmy and perhaps allow them to come round to my house to see him again.

'As you know, Jimmy's six months old now and we really need to start setting out a long-term plan for his future,' she said when she called round a few hours later.

'Of course,' I said, stirring the cup of tea I'd just made her. 'That's understandable.'

'I've spent the last few weeks talking to my manager, Jimmy's guardian Douglas and the other people involved in this case to see what they feel the best option would be for Jimmy, moving forward,' she said. 'We've weighed it all up and we're going to be holding a case conference with the legal department next week.'

'Yes, we were due to have a case conference last month but it was postponed for a few weeks to see how this new contact went,' I said. 'Are you allowed to give me any information about what your thoughts might be, or what you're leaning towards?

'I've always thought a family residential assessment would be ideal and I've been pushing for that since the beginning,' I added.

'I'm afraid the general consensus seems to be that adoption would be the best option for Jimmy,' she said. 'That's probably what we'll be recommending to the court.'

At first I thought I'd misheard her.

'Adoption?' I gasped, nearly dropping my cuppa. 'But things have been going so well. Jess and Darren have proved their commitment. They've been going to contact even when they've been poorly and done everything that's been asked of them. They've really pulled their socks up.'

I was struggling to keep the emotion out of my voice.

'Yes, they have,' said Debbie. 'We're not disputing that. But this is more about their age and our concerns that they're not mature enough at this point to cope with being parents.'

'I'm afraid I have to disagree with you there,' I said. 'They might be young but together they make a strong team. They have a good relationship and they really support each other.'

'But they've never been on their own with a baby and that's a big difference,' said Debbie. 'Soon that baby's going to turn into a toddler and become more demanding and less compliant. Will they be able to cope with that and normal household duties such as cooking, cleaning and paying bills?

'They've shown us how they cope with pressure – they run. Jess left Jimmy in your care and went to live with Darren. When they thought he might be taken away they took him and disappeared. They react like impulsive teenagers.

'Do they know how to manage money? At the minute Social Services even pay their bus fares to get to and from contact.'

'They're all things they can learn in time,' I said desperately.

I'd been so hopeful that Debbie was going to believe in Jess and Darren and see what I saw, that they were good enough parents for Jimmy. This was a bitter blow.

'Unfortunately we haven't got time,' said Debbie. 'Jimmy can't hang around in the care system waiting for them to be mature enough. It's not in his best interests.'

'I honestly don't think this is the right decision,' I said. I had to be true to my feelings. I owed it to Jess and Darren to tell her that she was making a mistake. Now was not the time to stay silent.

'I know it's going to be very hard and distressing for them,' she said. 'But ultimately we believe in the long-term that it's the best thing for Jimmy.'

Debbie had organised a case conference for the following week at Social Services, where we would discuss the matter further.

'At the meeting everyone will get the chance to have their say, but ultimately I feel the best way forward is adoption rather than a residential assessment, and then obviously the legal department will weigh up whether they think there's enough evidence to take that to the family court.'

This was all a huge shock. To me, it sounded like the decision had already been made and it was just a case of legally signing it off.

'When are you going to tell Jess and Darren this?' I asked, my heart sinking.

Like me, I knew they wouldn't have seen this coming and were under the impression that things were going well and that they'd turned a corner with Social Services. This was going to devastate them.

'I wanted to speak to you first,' said Debbie. 'Now I'm going to go and see Jess and Darren and let them know about the meeting and inform them that we're looking at adoption as the best way forward for Jimmy.'

'Please could you ring me back once you've been to see them?' I asked. 'I'd like to know how they're doing.'

'Of course,' she said.

I knew this was their worst fear, and I felt utterly shocked and saddened that it was becoming a reality.

Debbie called me back a couple of hours later.

'How did they take it?' I asked.

'As expected,' she sighed. 'Jess was absolutely distraught and Darren was upset and very angry. There was lots of shouting and swearing and threatening not to come to the meeting.

'However, I explained that the meeting would take place whether or not they attended and that it was advisable for them to come with their solicitor.'

A few minutes after I'd put the phone down to Debbie, Jess called. I hadn't got permission for phone calls with her, just texts, but I knew I couldn't not answer it after the bombshell that had just been dropped on them.

She was hysterical.

'Maggie, they're going to take Jimmy away,' she sobbed. 'They're really doing it.'

There was nothing I could say to reassure her any more. We'd reached the end of the line.

'I don't understand,' she said between huge gasps of air. 'Me and Daz have tried so hard. We've done everything they wanted. Why are they doing this to us now?'

'It's just a recommendation. Let's see what actually happens at the meeting,' I said. 'Your solicitor will be there and he can help argue your case, and I'll tell them what I think.'

'I think it's too late – they're gonna take him,' she shrieked, her voice rising with hysteria. 'I just know it.'

'Don't give up yet,' I said, trying to soothe her.

'It's no use,' she sobbed. 'We've lost him. We've lost our baby, Maggie.'

It was heart-wrenching to hear her so upset. However, I also had to make it clear to her that I would have to let Becky know that she'd called me.

'You've got to remember that I'm Jimmy's carer and not yours any more. There's nothing wrong with you ringing me and being upset, I just have to make sure that I log it and cover my back.'

'I understand,' she told me, sounding so sad and resigned. 'I just needed to call you cos I felt so sad. I don't know what to do any more.'

'Talk to your solicitor,' I urged her.

Afterwards I called Becky and told her what had happened.

'Was there anything Jess said that gives you cause for concern?' she asked.

'No,' I said. 'There were no threats to Jimmy or anything to give me reason to think she might do something stupid. She was genuinely upset.'

I was choked up about it too. Even though I'd worked with a lot of parents over the years, you can't help but get affected when you've looked after a mum and her baby who you know ultimately are going to be separated.

That night, as I put Jimmy to bed, I had a tear in my eye as I thought about Jess and Darren and how desperate they must have been feeling. How on earth do you say goodbye to your child? I couldn't even begin to imagine how that must feel.

'What's going to happen to you, little man?' I sighed as I kissed him goodnight. 'Where are you going to end up?'

The whole situation was so genuinely sad for everyone.

Even when you know it's the correct decision it's still hard, but in this case all my instincts were screaming that this wasn't right. I understood their upset and Darren's anger. I'd be angry too if someone was trying to take my child away from me, no matter how old I was. But was there really anything I could do at this stage to stop it?

On the morning of the meeting I dropped Jimmy off with my friend Vicky. Case conferences were very formal and I needed to listen and concentrate – it would be too distracting for everyone having a young baby there. Plus it wouldn't be fair on Jess and Darren; their sense of loss and fear was great enough as it was, without Jimmy being there to remind them of what they stood to lose.

'How are you feeling about today?' asked Vicky, as I handed Jimmy over in his car seat.

'To be honest, a bit nervous,' I said. 'I'm nervous about how Darren and Jess are going to react. Darren can be volatile at the best of times. Also my gut is telling me that they're making a terrible mistake and that this is the wrong decision.'

'Well, if that's what you believe then you have to say something,' she told me.

However, as a foster carer, to stick your head above the parapet and go against what everyone else was saying was an extremely hard thing to do. There were lots of people at this meeting who no doubt I would come across again and have to work with in the future – they'd now see me as a troublemaker. But I knew I couldn't just sit there and let something happen that I was so strongly against.

I met Becky in Social Services' reception and we went up to the meeting room. Everyone who had been involved in the case was attending and we were all sitting round a large table. Debbie was there, Martin her manager, Douglas the guardian, Jimmy's health visitor, myself and Becky, two members of the Social Services legal department and an admin person who would take notes. I'd just sat down when Jess and Darren arrived with their solicitor.

Jess gave me a weak smile as she came in and saw me. She looked exhausted like she hadn't slept, and her eyes were red and puffy from crying. She looked like a frightened little girl. Darren was sullen and didn't say anything as they sat down.

Kimberly, the Independent Review Officer, was chairing the meeting. She went through what had been happening, how Darren and Jess had taken Jimmy and how new contact was in place, and she read statements from the health visitor and the psychologist. Then it was Debbie's turn to speak.

'We need to put a long-term plan in place for Jimmy, and on balance, we feel adoption is the best way forward.'

I looked over at Jess. She started to cry and Darren had his head in his hands.

'There's no doubt in my mind that these parents love their child,' said Douglas the guardian. 'But that's not the issue here. The issue is that they're sixteen and seventeen – they're children themselves, and I don't feel that they'd be able to meet the ongoing needs of a child and cope with the pressures of day-to-day family life.'

Kimberly went round the table and every single person agreed with the recommendation for adoption. As each one spoke, Jess sank further and further down in her seat, sobbing. I could see her crumbling in front of my eyes, and I was worried she was going to collapse onto the floor.

'I know this must be upsetting and very hard for you to hear,' Kimberly told her. 'Would you like a glass of water?'

Jess shook her head, her bottom lip trembling.

Even from over the other side of the table, I could feel the anger building up inside Darren. I could see the tension in his body language. His fists were clenched and his face was getting redder and redder.

Keep it together, I willed him. *Don't say anything you'll regret later.*

Having an outburst would do him no favours whatsoever. But he was like a volcano about to erupt, and seeing Jess so upset was the final straw.

'Look what you've done to her,' he shouted. 'Why are you taking our baby away from us?'

'Darren, we're here to gather information so we can make a recommendation to the court to do what we believe is in Jimmy's best interests,' Debbie told him.

'And you think it's best to take him away from us,' he sneered. 'You're all the bloody same. You're just as bad as that bitch Katherine.'

'I'm sorry, Darren, but we're not willing to put up with shouting or that sort of language in this meeting,' Kimberly said. 'If you carry on then I'm afraid we'll have to call security and ask you to leave.'

'You don't have to ask me to leave cos I'm f***ing well going,' he yelled.

He got up and stormed out, slamming the door behind him. Jess buried her head in her hands and wept. My heart sank. This was all we needed.

'Excuse me for a moment,' said their solicitor, going out after him.

Five minutes later, Darren and the solicitor came back into the room. Darren looked very sheepish and the solicitor had obviously had a word with him and told him what to say.

'I'm very sorry,' he told Kimberly. 'My emotions got the better of me.'

The meeting resumed. Everyone else had given their opinion and now I knew it was my turn.

'What do you think, Maggie?' Kimberly asked me.

'Before I tell you what I think, you have to bear in mind that I'm one of the only people who has seen the three of them together in an informal setting,' I said.

I took a deep breath.

'I honestly feel that adoption isn't the best option for Jimmy,'

I told them. 'Jess and Darren love their son, and I believe that together, with the right support, they have the ability to be good parents to Jimmy, and that it's in his best interests to keep them together.'

Everyone was staring at me but I carried on.

'All along Jess and Darren have been saying that they want to be a family. So let's find them a residential unit where they can be together and be assessed as a family. I think they deserve to have that chance,' I said.

'From what I can gather they've had lots of chances,' said Debbie. 'A family residential assessment will take more time, and if that fails, that's more time Jimmy will have spent in the care system. Time that could be spent finding an adoptive family and settling him in.

'Plus, a residential assessment was something that was discussed and then ruled out by the previous social worker.'

'With all due respect, Debbie, I don't think the previous social worker was willing to work with Jess and Darren, and I don't believe she gave enough thought to a residential assessment,' I said.

'I understand, like with most things, that there are financial implications, but costs aside, this is what I feel is in Jimmy's best interests – not adoption.'

Afterwards I felt relieved that I'd spoken my mind. It had been hard to go against what everyone else was saying and perhaps put my professional reputation in jeopardy, but in my heart of hearts I knew I'd done the right thing.

'I agree with Maggie,' said Darren. 'Why can't me and Jess live together with Jimmy and see how we get on?'

His solicitor put his hand on Darren's arm as if to signal for him not to say any more.

'Can I ask why this option can't be explored again for my clients?' the solicitor asked.

'Because if it doesn't work then we're right back to square one,' said Debbie. 'Plus their track record of co-operating with Social Services and being committed to contact isn't exactly good. It's only in the past month that they've started to co-operate.'

'I'd urge you to look at this option again for my clients' sake,' he told them. 'After that there would be no more chances.'

Kimberly nodded and shuffled her papers.

'OK, we need to talk to legal and make a decision about how we're going to proceed,' she said. 'So could the birth parents and the foster carer please wait outside?'

We weren't allowed to be involved in any legal discussions. We went out into the corridor; I sat down on a plastic chair next to Jess and put my arm around her. She collapsed against me, howling like a mortally wounded animal.

'They're going to take my baby away,' she cried, her blue eyes filled with fear.

'I'm so, so sorry,' I said. 'I did what I could. Your solicitor will do his best to push for further assessments and you never know, perhaps the court will listen. It's not over yet. Get him to look into residential homes and explore all of the options. Don't give up.'

I knew I'd probably said too much and shouldn't say any more. There was a fine line between supporting Jess and Darren and going against Social Services. I had a responsibility as Jimmy's carer, and I knew that whatever decision came from the case conference I would have to support it.

Time ticked on. Fifteen minutes passed and there was still no news from the meeting room. Darren went outside for a cigarette and Jess and I sat there waiting. There wasn't a lot I could say to reassure her.

'Where's Jimmy today?' she asked.

'He's at my friend Vicky's house,' I said. 'She's looking after him.'

'He'll be having his sleep now, won't he?' She smiled, looking at the time on her phone.

She chatted normally for a few minutes and then a fresh batch of tears fell as she thought about what was going to happen.

It was half an hour before the meeting room door opened and Kimberly poked her head out.

'Would you like to come back in now?' she asked.

She looked over at Jess and saw the fresh tears wetting her face.

'Are you OK?' she asked. 'Sorry to keep you waiting. I know this is terribly distressing for you, so we won't keep you much longer.'

When everyone had sat down Kimberly began. 'OK, we've talked to legal and we've reached a decision.'

I took a deep breath and closed my eyes. I felt sick with nerves. Had they listened to my concerns, or would Jess and Darren soon be forced to say goodbye to their son? Were their dreams of being a happy family about to be shattered?

THIRTEEN

Second Chances

My heart was thumping out of my chest as I waited for Kimberly to speak. I couldn't look at Jess but I could hear her quietly sobbing.

'We've decided to go to court and apply for a full care order as well as a freeing order so that Jimmy can be placed for adoption.'

I shook my head, my heart sinking. I felt utterly defeated.

'No!' Jess whimpered. 'You can't do this to us.'

'You're not taking our son away. You ain't having him!' yelled Darren.

'I know this information is very distressing for you both, but you'll be able to talk to your solicitor about it afterwards,' Kimberly told them.

'Thank you all for attending.'

She closed her notebook and with that everyone started packing away.

'I need to go,' I told Becky. 'I have to pick up Jimmy.'

It might seem harsh, but I wanted to get out of that room as quickly as possible. The truth was I didn't know what to say to Jess and Darren. And I didn't know if I would be able to contain my own emotions. I could see their pain but there was nothing I could do or say any more to make it better.

Jess was sobbing in Darren's arms.

I put my hand on her shoulder.

'I'm so sorry, Jess, love. I've got to go now and pick up Jimmy,' I told her. 'But make sure you talk to your solicitor.'

She nodded through her tears.

As Becky and I got into the lift she could see that I was upset.

'Are you all right, Maggie?' she asked.

'Not really,' I sighed. 'I'm finding it difficult to be part of a team who are taking a baby away from his parents when my gut is telling me it's not right.'

'You told them your views,' she said. 'Unfortunately there's not a lot more you can do – now it's in the court's hands.'

It was so frustrating. Nothing brought the implications of that decision home to me more than when I walked into Vicky's house and saw Jimmy sitting in a high chair having his lunch. His chubby little cheeks were smeared with yogurt and he was noisily banging his beaker on the plastic tray. When he saw me come in, he gave me a big grin. Little did he know that a room full of strangers had just decided that his future wasn't to be with his birth parents.

'How did it go?' Vicky asked.

I shook my head.

'They've decided to go for adoption,' I told her. 'I'm gutted, Vicky. I really am.'

'But we've looked after lots of mums who've had their babies removed,' she said. 'And although it's sad we've always known it's the right thing to happen.'

'Yes, but this doesn't feel like the right decision,' I said.

'Unfortunately that's the hard part of being a foster carer,' said Vicky. 'We have to follow what the social workers want us to do.'

I believe that, wherever possible, families should be kept together, and children should only be taken away if every possible option has been explored. But in this case I didn't feel like it had.

'By the way, how's Lily doing?' Vicky asked.

'Great,' I said. 'She's enjoying seeing more of her mum, and it seems to be going really well. There's a meeting in a couple of weeks about the plan to return her home.'

'That's brilliant,' said Vicky.

I was involved in two very different scenarios – Jimmy was facing losing his birth mother and Lily was being reunited with hers after several years of living apart. I wondered how differently their lives were going to turn out because of the change in their circumstances.

In the days after the case conference everything carried on as normal, including contact. When I picked Jimmy up from the contact centre, Lesley was there to meet me.

'Mum's really struggling,' she said. 'She's been very weepy and clingy with the baby today. I heard what happened at the meeting last week. Poor kid.'

'It's really hit her hard,' I said.

Debbie rang me a couple of days later. 'How are you, Maggie?' she asked. 'How's Jimmy?'

'We're fine, thanks,' I said.

I knew there was no point being difficult with her. I'd shared my views at the case conference and now I had to let it go.

Like everyone involved in this case, I had to work towards the agreed plan, and there was nothing to be gained from airing my disappointment and upset again.

'I wanted to let you know there's going to be a directions hearing next week,' Debbie told me.

This was a closed hearing in the family court where Social Services put their plans for Jimmy in front of a judge and he or she decided whether this was the right option to take. Darren and Jess would attend court with their solicitor and Social Services' legal team would be there, along with Debbie and Douglas, Jimmy's guardian.

'In the meantime I've spoken to the adoption team and someone should be ringing you in the next couple of weeks,' she said. 'We want to start putting together some information about Jimmy so we can see what families are out there for him.

'It would also be helpful if you could sort some photos of Jimmy out so we can start putting a storybook together about him that can be shown to potential adopters.'

'No problem,' I said.

My job was about working with Social Services and I had to respect that, but inside I felt very sad that the wheels of adoption were being put in motion. However, I knew my sadness was nothing compared to what Jess and Darren must be feeling right now.

Jess texted every day to ask how Jimmy was.

He's fine, I wrote. *How are you?*

Not great. I'm crying a lot and the doctor has put me on some tablets. We're talking to our solicitor. Daz says we can fight this but I ain't sure. I think we've lost him.

All I could reply was *I'm thinking about you x*

The following week it was time for the directions hearing. That morning I took Jimmy upstairs for his nap. As I zipped him into his sleeping bag and put him down in the cot, I couldn't help but wonder what today held for him. While it was an ordinary morning for us, a few miles away a judge who we'd never met was deciding on his future. As usual, I threw myself into cleaning the house to try and distract myself. I made sure I had my mobile by my side as I'd asked Debbie to call me afterwards.

She rang just as I'd stopped to make some lunch.

'Well?' I asked. 'How did it go?'

'I'm actually on my way round to see you now,' she said. 'So I'll explain to you then.'

'Oh, OK,' I said, heart sinking.

I knew from the fact that she was coming round that something major must have happened at court. All sorts of terrible scenarios ran through my mind. Had Darren kicked off, or done something stupid like threaten the judge? *Oh, please God don't let them have arrested him*, I thought. Or was it Jess? Had she collapsed or gone missing again?

By the time Debbie arrived I'd driven myself mad with worry.

'What is it?' I asked as soon as she walked in. 'What on earth happened at court?'

'Well, let's just say things didn't exactly go according to plan,' she told me.

'Oh, no,' I sighed, feeling sicker by the minute. 'In what way?'

'All I can say is that Jess and Darren seem to have got themselves a very good solicitor.'

'What do you mean?' I said.

'He put a very convincing argument to the judge about how the previous social worker had been biased and how he didn't feel that we'd fully explored every option. The judge wants to put plans for a care order on hold and instead would like us to go away and relook at the possibility of doing a residential family assessment.'

'What?' I gasped, my face breaking into a smile of relief.

'I must admit it was quite a surprise to me but he shared your views, Maggie. He said that if Jess and Darren had continually asked to be a family then we should assess them as a family unit and see how they get on.

'That assessment would be carried out by people who haven't previously been involved in the case, so it would be completely unbiased.'

'I honestly don't believe it,' I said. 'That's brilliant news.'

It was what Jess and Darren had wanted all along, and now someone had actually listened to them.

'It's obviously not the outcome that we had pushed for, however, I have to respect the judge's opinion and follow through with his recommendations,' said Debbie.

'How did Jess and Darren react?' I asked.

'Oh, as you can imagine they were ecstatic,' she said. 'They went from despair to jubilation in a matter of seconds.

'The judge told them in no uncertain terms that this was their very last chance. They know they're incredibly lucky to get this assessment and that if it fails, then Jimmy will automatically be placed for adoption.'

My head was still reeling as Debbie explained they'd be looking at a twelve-week assessment.

'If it's not going well then it can be cancelled at any point,' she said. 'We're going to start looking at suitable residential facilities, but as you know it may take a while for a place to become available.'

Mother-and-baby units were common, but units where whole families could live together were few and far between.

While Debbie was explaining all this to me, I was doing a silent jig of glee inside my head for Jess and Darren.

They'd got what they wanted at last. Now all I could hope was that they didn't mess it up.

The judge's recommendation had taken everyone at Social Services by surprise. Now instead of reducing contact leading up to Jimmy's adoption, they needed to start increasing it. At the moment Jimmy was only used to seeing Jess and Darren twice a week for a couple of hours. He was seven months old, and he was coming up to the age where he was starting to get clingy with me as I was his main carer. At a residential centre they'd be living with each other 24/7, so they needed to build up their relationship with him again. If they didn't then it could be disastrous and they'd start the assessment at a disadvantage.

'We'll still keep the two contact sessions, but we're going to add in a couple of extra sessions back at the family centre,' said Debbie. 'Eventually we'll build it up to five days a week.'

Even by the time Debbie left, I was still shocked by the massive turnaround. I'd expected to be talking through the schedule for adoption and the emotional process of Darren and Jess saying goodbye to their son for ever. Now plans were being put in place so that all three of them could live together.

Jess called me half an hour later, and she sounded like a different person.

'Have you heard, Maggie?' she asked.

'Debbie's just been round and told me what happened at court,' I said.

'We did it!' she said. 'I can't believe it. The judge listened to us and he's letting us all live together. I'm so happy, Maggie. I can't wait to see Jimmy and cuddle him.'

She sounded so happy and relieved, I hated to burst her bubble. But she was talking like they were off the hook.

'I'm really pleased for you both,' I said. 'But remember, you've still got to pass the assessment. Nothing is guaranteed.'

'I know,' she said. 'Don't worry, we will.'

When I rang Becky and told her what was going on, I discussed my concerns.

'They're acting like they've won the Lottery and I'm utterly delighted for them,' I said. 'But I hope they realise how hard this assessment is going to be.

'The family centre assessment will seem like a walk in the park compared to what they'll have to do. I just hope they can cope with it.'

'Well, if they can't it will soon become apparent,' said Becky.

Contact at the family centre started straight away and, like before, I was able to drop Jimmy off and pick him up. It was the first time I'd seen Jess and Darren since the directions hearing.

Jess rushed over to me as soon as I walked in. She threw her arms around me and gave me a massive hug, then she plucked Jimmy out of his car seat.

'We're going to be together at last, little man,' she said, dancing around with him in her arms. 'We're going to be a family – you, me and Daddy.

'I still can't believe it, Maggie,' she told me. 'They finally listened to us.'

'I'm delighted for all three of you,' I said.

'When it's all finished, Daz will have turned eighteen so that means we can get a council house.'

Jess was full of plans for the future. I didn't want to bring her back down to earth, but it was important to be realistic. At the end of the day things could still go wrong, the assessment could fail and Jimmy would be placed for adoption. But they hadn't even thought about that possibility.

Darren was on cloud nine too.

'I'm sorry if I was rude at the meeting the other week,' he said. 'I was angry and felt like no one was listening to us.'

'It's OK,' I said. 'It's understandable that you were both very upset.'

I left them to it, hoping beyond hope that they really were up to the challenge, as this truly was their last chance to be Jimmy's parents.

A couple of weeks after the directions hearing, Debbie phoned me with an update.

'There's a possible place coming up in six weeks' time at a family assessment centre twenty miles away,' she said. 'They'd have to go for an interview there to check they're suitable, but it looks ideal.'

'That's amazing,' I said.

These types of units were few and far between, so it was possible they may have had to travel anywhere in the country to get a place.

'Contact is going really well, but we need to build it up to five days a week as soon as we can,' she said.

The issue now was that neither the contact centre nor the family centre had any availability.

'Would you consider doing what we did early on in the placement, and allow Darren and Jess to come to my house?' I asked. 'I could make them tea and then they could stay and help put Jimmy to bed. It would be good to get them involved in his bedtime routine again.'

'If you're happy to do that then I don't see why not,' she said. 'They've been co-operating with us, and you'll obviously be there to supervise them.'

The girls were delighted when I told them that Jess and Darren were coming round, as they hadn't seen either of them for months.

'What's happening now?' Louisa asked. 'Is Jimmy still going back to live with them?'

'I'll let Jess explain it all to you if she wants to,' I said.

Lily, meanwhile, was busy setting up the Monopoly board in time for Darren's visit.

'I'm definitely going to beat him.' She smiled.

Jess and Darren seemed happy to be back doing contact at my house.

'I've missed your dinners, Maggie,' said Darren as he tucked into sausage and mash.

I made sure I kept a close eye on them, and was pleased to see they were very natural with Jimmy and knew what they were doing. The bond between them and Jimmy had grown too, and he held his arms out to them and got upset when Jess left the room, which was a good sign.

However, although they were very relaxed at my house, I knew the assessment unit was going to test them to the limits. It would be a huge challenge for them, and I wanted them to be prepared.

Debbie had arranged to come round and see them one evening at my house.

'We've hopefully found you a place at a family residential centre that starts in six weeks,' she told them.

'You'll have a chance to go and look round it before you move and meet the staff and check you're happy, and they want to interview you too. In the meantime, I wanted to reiterate that if this place does happen then this is your very last chance.

'I need to be very honest with you here and make sure you're aware that if you mess this up, there won't be any more chances and we will be going down the adoption route. We're putting the care order on hold until the end of the twelve-week assessment. By then the centre will have decided whether your parenting is good enough or not.

'If there are any doubts, then the assessment can be extended to up to twenty-four weeks.'

'We might have to live there for six months?' gasped Darren.

'Yes, if the residential centre feels that you're not quite ready and there's more work to be done, then they can ask you to remain there longer,' she told them.

Both Jess and Darren looked horrified.

'You've got this chance to prove yourselves, so please don't waste it,' Debbie urged them.

'I promise you we won't,' said Jess. 'We know if we mess this up Jimmy's going to be taken off us, and we won't let that happen.'

Finally they seemed to be taking things seriously.

Before Debbie left, she had a quiet word with me.

'How do you think they're doing, now contact is up to five days a week?' she asked.

'I really think that they've matured,' I said. 'They came so close to losing Jimmy, and I think that shocked them into finally taking responsibility and acting like his parents.'

I could see it in little things, like the fact that Darren didn't go outside for a cigarette until after Jimmy was in bed, whereas before he was in and out all the time. They didn't ask me to help care for Jimmy when they were both together at my house, they just got on with it.

As time passed, there was also the realisation that I was going to have to say goodbye to Jimmy. He'd been in our lives since he was three days old, and all of us had grown to love this little boy. But any sadness that we felt was overtaken by the fact that he had the chance to live with his biological parents, which was the best-case scenario. At the back of my mind, I was also very aware that soon, if everything went well, I'd be saying goodbye to Lily too. I could see that Jimmy going had made her think about leaving us.

I overheard her playing with Jimmy one day.

'We've got to be really kind to Maggie,' she told him. 'Because soon we're both going to live with our mummies and she's going to be really sad.'

She was right. It was going to be a huge wrench to say goodbye to a baby I loved as well as a little girl who, after four years, I'd come to view as my own. The next few weeks were going to be testing – for all of us.

FOURTEEN

Routines and Rules

A few days later, Debbie arranged to take Jess and Darren to visit the residential centre. They had to have an interview to check that they were suitable before they formally offered them a place, and they needed to have a look round to check they were happy with the centre.

'They'd like to meet Jimmy, too, so would it be possible for you to bring him down?' she asked me.

'Of course,' I said. 'I don't mind driving him over there.'

As I pulled up into the unit's car park, Debbie, Darren and Jess were already there.

'I'll wait in the car while you all go in,' I said, handing Jimmy to Jess. 'Text me when you want me to come and get him.'

As the baby's foster carer, it wasn't necessary for me to go and look round or sit in on any meetings – I wouldn't normally be allowed to for confidentiality reasons.

Jess looked at Debbie pleadingly.

'Can't Maggie come too?' she asked. 'I'd really like her to come in with us.'

I could tell she was apprehensive and not sure what to expect, and perhaps me being there would help reassure her.

'I don't see why not,' said Debbie. 'Maggie's been involved in your case from day one, and I'm sure she'll keep any information confidential.'

To be honest, I was pleased, as I was intrigued to see the centre and find out what Darren and Jess would be expected to do. Most placements I'd had in the past had tended to be with mother-and-baby units, and I hadn't dealt with this particular family unit before.

From the outside, the centre looked like a large, grand Victorian house. A path of original tiles led up to a huge wooden front door with ornate stained-glass panels. We rang the bell and a woman in jeans and a jumper came to meet us.

'I'm Hannah McGarry,' she said. 'I'm the manager here.'

We all introduced ourselves, and, much to Jess and Darren's bemusement, she shook everyone's hands.

'Come in and I'll show you around,' she said, leading us into a large hallway with high ceilings and a gleaming wooden banister.

'This is lovely,' Debbie whispered to me.

It felt like walking into a family home, and the rooms were huge. We went into the living room first. Even though it was April, it was still chilly outside and the fire was on and there were squishy sofas and cushions, so it was all very cosy.

'This is the playroom,' she said, taking us next door. It was a bright, sunny room with shelves full of toys, paints, crayons and books. There were beanbags on the floor and the walls were covered with children's artwork.

'This is where parents and their children can come and play and we do group play therapy work in here,' she said.

'It's dead nice,' said Jess. 'Jimmy will love all the toys.'

She showed us the laundry room where everyone did their washing and the communal kitchen with a long table at one end.

'You'll have a small kitchen in your own flat where you can cook, but once a week the residents help cook a meal and eat it all together in here,' she said.

Then she showed us into a smaller room that looked more like an office.

'This is where we have our therapy sessions,' she told us. 'It can be one-to-one sessions, or couples or family therapy.'

'What do you have to do in therapy?' asked Darren suspiciously.

'Sometimes parents like to talk to someone about how it feels to be a mum or dad, or to talk about their relationship with their partner or any worries that they might have,' she explained.

'I don't want to talk to no stranger about private things,' he said. 'I ain't very good at talking.'

'A lot of people think that when they first come, but then they try it and find that it really helps,' Hannah told him, although Darren didn't look convinced.

'I'll take you upstairs and show you the flats now,' she said.

While downstairs had been very cosy and homely, upstairs was a stark contrast.

'There are three individual flats, so we can have up to three families here at a time.'

She showed us into one. It was very small and poky, and one big room had been divided off to make different spaces. There was a tiny lounge with an open-plan kitchen in one corner. It was very bare and minimal and smelt of air freshener. There were no sofas, just three uncomfortable-looking wooden armchairs covered in tatty blue fabric like you'd find in an office, and a very rough industrial carpet on the floor. The basics were all there – there was a small dining table and two chairs, a fridge and a cooker. The bedroom was tiny and had a double bed, a wardrobe and a chest of drawers in it, and then there was a small box room next to it with a cot.

'You'll need to bring your own TV if you want one, and you'll need towels and bedding for yourself and the baby,' said Hannah.

Jess looked anxious.

'I ain't got no bedding,' she whispered to me.

'Don't worry,' I said. 'I've got plenty that you can have.'

The flat was very bare and cold with a flimsy, draughty window overlooking the main road outside. There were no little touches to make it cosy, like lamps or pictures or rugs, and what furniture there was was well used and tatty. However, Jess and Darren seemed to love it.

'Look, Daz, we've got our own kitchen.' Jess grinned. 'There's a cooker and everything.'

'It's dead nice, innit,' he said.

They were so happy to finally have a space of their own – they didn't care about home comforts and knick-knacks.

After the tour, Hannah took us down to the office. Jess and Darren had to fill in some paperwork and questionnaires, and be interviewed by members of staff to check they were suitable for the assessment.

While they were doing that, Hannah took Debbie and me to one side.

'I need to make sure that before Jess and Darren commit to coming here they have a clear understanding of the rules,' she said. 'I'd like to talk you through them as well, so that you can reiterate them over the next couple of weeks.

'We have a zero-tolerance policy to alcohol, which isn't allowed in the building, and neither is smoking.

'Any acts of aggression or violence towards our staff will not be tolerated and if that happens then the assessment will be terminated with immediate effect and they'll be asked to leave.'

She also talked us through the supervision and how it would work.

'I'm not going to lie to you or them,' she said. 'It's tough going, and they need to be fully committed to it. They'll be supervised twenty-four hours a day, seven days a week for the first few weeks, and they're not allowed to be on their own with Jimmy.

'They're not allowed to leave the centre on their own with Jimmy, and if they go out individually then they need to let someone know where they are at all times.'

She explained that, for the first four weeks, Jess and Darren would be observed by two members of staff. If that went well then it would eventually be reduced to one person.

'If we have any doubts or worries then we can extend any of the supervision periods if we think they need it,' she said. 'The staff need to be confident that they can trust them with the baby.

'They'll be observed in everything they do with Jimmy, from giving him a bottle to bathing, dressing and playing with him, and the supervisors will make detailed notes.

'At 8 p.m. every night a member of staff will come up to the flat and go through their report from that day with them. They'll talk through what they saw, what they evidenced, what they liked and what they think needs to be changed.'

She also explained how they had to do a shopping list and come up with a meal plan each week, which would be gone through by a worker who'd teach them how to budget.

'We do a very thorough, comprehensive assessment here,' Hannah told us. 'There will be reports from psychologists, doctors and play therapists.

'Every day Jess and Darren will have a full timetable, from group play sessions and therapy to working with a dietician learning about healthy food and diets.

'There's not much free time or privacy. They will have their own flat, but the door must never be locked so that staff can have access at all times.'

It all sounded extremely stressful, and it was going to be a massive challenge for Jess and Darren.

'How do you think they'll cope?' Debbie asked me when Hannah left the room. 'My worry is how Darren will react. He sometimes has problems with authority and being told what to do,' she continued.

'It's going to be hard for them,' I said. 'To be honest, I think most of us would find it hard being watched and monitored by strangers twenty-four hours a day. But they know this is their last chance, and that for Jimmy's sake they have to make this work.'

'Darren will have to learn to accept criticism and hold his tongue,' agreed Debbie.

'He'll have to,' I said. 'Otherwise it's game over.'

Debbie stayed at the centre with Jess and Darren so that they could fill in some forms while I drove back home with Jimmy. A couple of hours later Debbie dropped them back at mine, as they were due round for tea. They were both very quiet and looked shell-shocked.

'How did it go?' I asked Debbie when they'd gone into the living room to see Jimmy.

'The good news is they were offered a place,' she said. 'The unit has given them twenty-four hours to think about whether they want to accept it.'

'What if they don't?' I asked.

'Then Jimmy will be placed for adoption,' she said.

So it wasn't really a choice as such.

'I think seeing the place and finding out how it's going to work has made them realise how hard it's going to be,' said Debbie. 'They knew they would have to be supervised, but I don't think they were expecting two people observing them 24/7.'

When Debbie had left, I asked them how they felt it had gone.

'OK,' sighed Jess. 'I liked the flat, but it's going to be really hard.'

'We're going to have two people watching us all the time,' said Darren. 'They'll even be checking that we can change a nappy. I said that was stupid, cos we've been changing Jimmy's nappies for months and we don't need no one to check.'

I was worried that Darren was moaning about it already.

'Darren, these staff don't know you, so the quicker you prove to them you can change a nappy or give Jimmy a bottle, the quicker it will be changed to just one person watching you,' I said.

'Well, I think it's stupid and a waste of time,' he said. 'It's like they don't trust us.'

'Why should they trust you?' I said. 'They don't know you. That's the whole point of this assessment – to prove to them that you can do it. They're watching you all the time to see how you respond to Jimmy and how he responds to you.

'Just go along with it and don't make it into a problem before you've even started.'

'They're really strict about Darren going for a ciggy too,' said Jess.

As well as Darren having to go outside to smoke, he'd been told that when he came back in, he had to change his clothes and then he wasn't allowed to hold Jimmy for an hour afterwards.

'That's really over the top, Maggie, ain't it?' he said.

I couldn't help but feel annoyed with him. After everything that had happened, they were lucky to even be getting this final chance.

'There's no point complaining before you even get there,' I said, struggling to keep the frustration from my voice. 'You have to suck it up and do whatever's required of you.'

'But, Maggie, it's just that . . .'

'Remember, this is exactly what you asked for, Darren,' I told him firmly. 'It's what you and Jess have been fighting for since the beginning, so don't mess it up.'

'We won't,' said Jess. 'Will we, Daz? We're not moaning, honest.'

He nodded, but I hoped she was right. The signs weren't good if Darren was kicking off even before they'd started living there.

'I can understand what you're saying,' I said. 'I've changed millions of nappies over the years, but even I would get nervous changing one if two people were watching me and taking notes.

'It would be really intimidating. But you have to do it because we all know what the alternative is.

'Remember, no one's forcing you to go,' I told them. 'It has to be your decision. You've been offered a place, and now you have to go away and think hard about whether you want to accept it.'

'What if we don't?' asked Jess.

'Then Jimmy will be placed for adoption,' I said.

'Well, we ain't got no choice then,' said Darren.

'Remember, you're good parents,' I told them. 'And once they're watching you with Jimmy, they'll realise that. You can do this.'

Jess gave me a weak smile.

'We'll give it a good try,' she said.

They accepted the place, and Debbie rang me a few days later.

'They can move in in a couple of weeks,' she said. 'The manager has advised that the best thing is if Jess and Darren move in a week before Jimmy.

'Then they can get settled into the flat, meet the workers, get to know their manager and key worker and the routine. They can also start some therapy sessions and group work before Jimmy arrives and the supervision starts.'

The plan was that I would take Jimmy to see them for a couple of hours each day and then he would go to live with them permanently a week later.

I was very aware that Jess and Darren had nothing to take with them, and I wanted to help them out. I sorted out four duvet covers that I said I didn't want as well as some cot bedding for Jimmy, and I bought them a couple of lamps to make the place homely as well as a couple of storage boxes for Jimmy's things. My friend Vicky gave them an old TV and my other foster carer friend Anne sorted out a pile of towels and tea towels. I bought some nice frames and printed out some photos of them with Jimmy so that they had something to put on the walls in the flat. By the end of the week, my dining room was filled with piles of stuff.

When they came round for tea one night, I showed them.

'What's all this?' asked Jess.

'It's for you to take to the residential centre,' I said. 'I thought you might need a few things.'

'Oh, Maggie,' she said, 'I dunno what to say. That's amazing, thank you.'

Darren didn't look that happy.

'I don't like accepting charity,' he said.

'When you've got your own place after you leave the residential centre and you have your own things, then you can give this stuff to charity and it can help someone else,' I said. 'We're just trying to help you and make the flat nice and comfortable for the three of you.'

The night before they were due to leave I invited them round for a goodbye tea with the girls.

'I know it's not really goodbye as I'll see you when I bring Jimmy down, so it's more of a good luck tea,' I said.

'Where are you going?' Lily asked them.

'Daz and I are going to live with Jimmy in our own flat,' Jess told her.

'Where is it?' Louisa asked, and Jess explained to her about the residential unit. For once, it was something that Louisa didn't know about and she seemed really interested in how it all worked.

'Maggie, we've got something to ask you,' Jess said shyly.

'Of course,' I said. 'What is it?'

'That Hannah lady said we're only allowed to choose one person to come and visit us while we're living at the residential centre. Daz and I were talking and we wanted it to be you.

'Would that be OK?' she asked. 'Would you mind coming to visit us? It don't have to be all the time. Just once or twice.'

'Of course I will, if that's what you both want,' I said. 'I'd love to come and see you. But don't you want your mum to come, Darren, or yours, Jess?'

'My mum don't give a toss where I'm going,' replied Darren. 'She says it's pointless, and Jimmy will be adopted anyway.'

'And my mum won't even answer the door to me so she's got no idea where I am,' said Jess.

'It would be an honour to come and see the three of you,' I said.

I felt so sad for both of them that they'd been so badly let down and rejected by their own parents. I was the closest thing they had to family. I knew how hard it had been for them to be parents when they hadn't had good parenting themselves, and I was proud of them for being so determined that Jimmy's childhood was going to be different to theirs. They desperately wanted their son to grow up knowing that he had two parents who loved him.

They both looked really touched when we gave them a 'good luck in your new home' card and the framed photos to go on the wall.

Before she left, Jess gave me a hug.

'I hope you enjoy your first day there and settle in OK,' I told her. 'Jimmy and I will see you the following day when we come to visit.'

She didn't say anything but I could feel her clinging onto me extra tightly and when she pulled away, she had tears in her eyes.

'What is it, sweetheart?' I asked.

'I'm scared, Maggie,' she said. 'What if I go to the centre and do something wrong? What if they think I'm a bad mum?'

'Nobody is perfect,' I told her. 'We all make mistakes, and everyone who works at the unit knows that. Remember, they're

202

not there to catch you out or see you fail. They're there to check Jimmy is safe and that you and Darren can look after him.

'Nobody knows everything. If they're saying something's not quite right, then explain to them why you were doing it and offer to change it. As long as you show willing and are prepared to work with them, you can't do any more.'

She looked up at me and nodded. Her eyes shone with tears.

'You're a good mum, Jess, and they will soon see that. So just do what they ask you, co-operate with them and believe in yourself.

'You can do this,' I told her. 'I know you can.'

'OK,' she sighed.

'And remember, you can text or ring me whenever you want and I'll come down and see you both.'

'I wish they could do the assessment here at your house instead of at the centre,' she sighed. 'It's going to be so weird, everyone watching us all the time.'

'I know,' I said. 'But we've been over this. It's only for a short time, and then you, Darren and Jimmy will have the rest of your lives to be a family. You've just got to get through the next twelve weeks.'

I could see that she was incredibly nervous. I really hoped with all my heart that she could do this. That my pep talk had helped, and that Darren would take criticism and learn to hold his tongue. Otherwise I knew the outcome. Little Jimmy would no longer be their son.

FIFTEEN

Under Pressure

Two days later I drove Jimmy down to the assessment centre to see Jess and Darren for the first time. I was keen to see how they were settling into their new flat. Even with all the things we'd given them, it still looked very sparse.

'How's it been?' I asked.

'It's OK,' said Jess. 'It feels a bit weird, but everyone seems nice.'

They'd done all the admin stuff like registering temporarily with the local doctor and signing on, but the twenty-four-hour supervision wouldn't kick in until Jimmy came to live with them. They made me a cup of tea in the flat and then we took Jimmy down to the playroom so he could meet the staff and get used to the space.

The next few days were strange for me as I spent them driving Jimmy back and forth to the centre. I'd packed up all of his things, and each day I brought some more of his stuff with me. I knew money was going to be very tight for Jess and Darren, so I'd done a few shopping trips and bought him some new clothes in bigger sizes so he'd have plenty. I'd sent a couple of big bags of toys from my house too so he'd have familiar things around him, as well as a big box of the washing powder that I used so his clothes would still smell the same to him.

'I can't wait to have him living with us again full-time,' Jess told me.

Her naivety worried me. I think they thought the moment they got him back everything would be normal – however, I suspected it was going to be a shock to the system for them. She hadn't lived with Jimmy full-time for months, and he needed a lot more stimulation now than he did when he was a tiny baby. He needed meals as well as milk and he needed to be played with. As typical teenagers who liked their sleep, I knew the early-morning wake-ups were going to be hard too. It was going to be tough for them to get used to doing all that at the same time as being observed and assessed.

On Jimmy's last day with me, I organised a little tea party at my house. Vicky and Anne came round with their foster children and they bought him a teddy, some books and 'good luck' cards.

Although Jimmy was too little to realise what was happening, it was important to mark a child's leaving and give them a proper goodbye for the sake of the other kids in my house who were left behind. Children often don't get a chance to say goodbye when they're taken into care and that can be very hard, so I always make sure the children I foster have this chance. Lily and Louisa had been used to kids coming and going over the years, but it always meant change and I knew they were going to miss Jimmy. Lily had made him a card and Louisa had bought him a wooden shape sorter from the pair of them.

'I know they're very good for a baby's development,' she told me, her love of her childcare course shining through.

'It's going to be strange without a baby in the house,' I sighed.

'I'm happy-sad about it,' said Lily. 'Sad he's going, but happy he's going to live with his mummy and daddy.'

'That's a very good way of putting it.' I smiled.

'How are you feeling about Jimmy going?' Vicky asked me when the kids were out of earshot and tucking into the buffet tea.

'To be honest I'm going to miss him dreadfully,' I said.

I'd fostered lots of babies over the years, and I always got attached to them and missed them when they left. But there were some with whom you really fell in love, and they captured a little piece of your heart. Jimmy was one of those babies.

'I know we all feel sad and miss the children when they leave, but the loss of Jimmy is going to run very deep. It's going to take me a while to get over it,' I said.

'It's understandable,' said Vicky. 'He's lived with you since he was two days old. You've been the one constant in his life.'

All she could do was give me a big hug as I fought to keep my emotions from surfacing.

The next morning Debbie came round to pick Jimmy up. The girls had said their goodbyes to him before they'd left for college and school.

'All set?' she asked.

'I think so,' I said.

I squeezed him tight and felt him cuddle into me for the last time.

'Goodbye, little man,' I whispered. 'I'm going to miss you so much.'

When I passed him to Debbie, he reached out his arms to me and started to cry.

'Don't worry,' I said, stroking his hair as she strapped him into the car seat. 'You're going to live with Mummy and Daddy. They can't wait to see you.'

Thankfully I managed to distract him with a toy and the tears eventually stopped.

'Before we go, Maggie, there's something I need to talk to you about,' said Debbie. 'Hopefully this won't happen, but I wanted to check with you just in case.'

I knew instantly what she was going to say.

'You want to know whether, if the assessment fails, I'd take Jimmy back, don't you?' I said. 'Well, the answer's yes. Hopefully it won't fail, but if the worst-case scenario happens then I'd be happy for him to come and live back here.'

'Thank you,' she said. 'I know it's a hard discussion to have but I just wanted to check.'

'No – it's important to have a plan in place, just in case,' I said.

I wanted Jess and Darren to succeed with all my heart, but if they failed the assessment and he wasn't able to live with them, then I hated the thought of Jimmy having to go and live with a stranger.

As Debbie walked down the path with Jimmy towards her car, I had a big lump in my throat.

'I'd better go in now and get on,' I called out.

Really it was because I wanted to shut the front door before the tears started to fall.

I can't lie – the next few days were hard. I missed Jimmy so much I had a physical ache. For the past seven months I'd loved and cared for him even when Jess was around, and he'd been permanently attached to my hip. My days had been filled with nappy changing, weaning, cuddling and playing. Now he'd gone, and the girls were at school and college, the house suddenly seemed very empty and quiet and I had all this free time on my hands. I couldn't accept another placement yet as I needed to wait and see what happened with the assessment and where Jimmy would be going at the end of the twelve weeks.

It wasn't just about missing a baby, though – it was about missing him and all his little habits. Like the way he stared up at me with his big blue eyes when I was giving him a bottle, never averting his gaze. Or the lovely way he snuggled into me when I held him.

I closed the door to his bedroom because it was hard to walk past and see it looking so bare without his stuff in there. But there were little reminders of him everywhere that would tug at my heartstrings: a tiny baby sock down the side of the sofa, a bag of rice cakes at the bottom of my handbag or a teething rattle I found in the drawer of my bedside table were all enough to trigger a pang of longing.

The silly thing about it was that I was the person who had championed this from the start. This was what I'd wanted for Jess, Darren and Jimmy, so I felt foolish for being so upset. Of course I was glad Jimmy was with his parents – but it didn't stop me from missing him.

As if I wasn't already feeling emotional enough, plans were starting to be put in motion for Lily to return to live with her mum full-time. For the past six months, Jane had had parenting assessments and counselling as well as spot checks to make sure she wasn't in contact with Lily's father. Things had gone well, and four days after Jimmy left there was a planning meeting at my house to discuss the transition period. Lily's social worker

Patricia was coming, along with Lily's mum Jane and Lily's Independent Review Officer, Kimberly. Lily had the same IRO as Jimmy, as children living in the same area tended to have the same person.

It was Kimberly who turned up first.

'How are you, Maggie?' she asked. 'I thought I'd come a little bit earlier so we could have a chat. How are you feeling now Jimmy's gone and Lily's likely to be going too?' she asked.

'It's been hard,' I said. 'I'm sad to see them go, but I know they'll both be in the right place.'

'Talking of Jimmy, how are Jess and Darren getting on?' she asked. 'Have you heard from them?'

'Not yet,' I said. 'They're not allowed to get in touch for the first week, so fingers crossed they're all OK. They're very committed and determined.'

'I really hope it works out for them,' she said. 'I know the assessment is going to be tough, but they fought so hard to go there.'

Everyone arrived and the meeting started. We talked about how over the next few weeks Lily's contact with her mum would be increased.

'Jane, it would be nice if instead of just having Lily for the weekend, you started picking her up from school on a Friday and then took her back with you,' said Patricia. 'Then we can gradually extend that to you having her until Monday morning and dropping her at school.'

'I've asked my boss about being a bit more flexible with my hours so they fit in with school pick-up and drop-off,' Jane told us.

Vicky had picked Lily up from school for me while we were having the meeting and she arrived back halfway through.

'Hi, Maggie,' said Lily, then she rushed over to see her mum and give her a cuddle. It was great how pleased Lily was to see her, and everyone could see the bond between them.

'We've just been talking about you going back to live with your mummy,' I told her.

'Would you like that?' Kimberly asked, and Lily nodded.

'Yes, but I'd like my bedroom to be pink before I move in,' she said.

'I'm sure I can sort that out.' Jane smiled.

I was really happy for Lily, but at the same time I was sad for myself. I also knew, though, that it wasn't going to be a permanent goodbye. Jane and I had built up a good relationship over the years and I'd already promised Lily that even when she left, she could still come to my house for tea once a week. Her mum's house was only a fifteen-minute drive away from us.

Even though I was dreading Lily going, the one thing the meeting did do was take my mind off Jess, Darren and Jimmy. It was hard not hearing from them – I couldn't help worrying and speculating about what was going on. Jess and Darren couldn't have visitors or even call or text anyone. They had to put all their energies into the assessment and settling in. I knew it was going to be very intense, and every day I thought about them and wondered how it was all going.

Exactly a week after I'd dropped Jimmy off, Jess rang me.

'How are you?' I asked. 'How's it going?'

'Oh, Maggie, it's horrible,' she said. She sounded like she was going to cry.

'We ain't got no privacy at all, we ain't ever on our own because there's two people watching us all the time.

'I had to hide behind a cupboard door to get dressed the other day cos people kept coming in our flat. They're meant to knock but they never do.

'We can't go for walk, and they listen in to everything me and Daz are saying. It's like being in prison, only I reckon prisoners get more rights than we do.'

She explained that at night they had to turn a baby monitor on that was connected to a twenty-four-hour reception downstairs.

'We don't dare speak in case they hear us talking,' she said.

'If Jimmy cries then we have to wait for someone to come up to watch us before we go into his bedroom and see him,' she said. 'The other night he woke up screaming and I was half asleep and I forgot I had to wait and I just went to him.

'I ended up getting a verbal warning for cuddling my own baby in the middle of the night. He was hysterical, Maggie. Don't you think that's stupid? Surely it means I'm a good mum, going to my baby if he's screaming the house down like that?'

'Oh, Jess,' I said. 'I understand how you're feeling, and I must admit I would find it really strange too. But you knew that this assessment was going to be extremely intrusive. It has to be – they're putting your parenting under the microscope.

'You've got to remember that it's just a short chapter in yours and Jimmy's lives and it will all be worth it in the end.'

'I know,' she sighed. 'It's just dead weird.'

'It sounds like you're doing brilliantly,' I said. 'Don't lose your temper, do whatever they ask of you and I'll come and see you in a week.

'Shall I bring the girls with me?' I asked.

'Yeah,' she said. 'That would be nice – if they want to come.'

As I was Darren and Jess's only named visitor, I'd been cleared by the assessment centre to come and see them once a fortnight. I'd also run it by Debbie, who was happy for me to visit.

'It will be good for them to have some contact with the outside world and see a friendly face,' she said.

I took down a chocolate cake and a pull-along train that I'd bought for Jimmy. Lily was excited about seeing him, and I think Louisa was intrigued to see the centre and how it worked. We all had to be signed in and I had to show my ID before one of the workers took us up to the flat.

'It's like being in a prison,' whispered Louisa.

Despite all the stress, Darren and Jess looked really well and the flat was clean and tidy.

'It's spotless in here,' I said.

'Yeah, well, we got a telling-off about keeping it clean and doing the washing, didn't we, Daz?' said Jess.

'They do spot checks to make sure,' he said. 'How was I supposed to know you're meant to empty your bins?'

'Well, that is what you'd have to do if you had your own house, Darren.' I smiled.

We all squeezed into the living room. There were only three chairs, so Lily and Louisa sat on the floor. Two women who I guessed were key workers were standing around. I said hello to them but neither of them said anything or introduced themselves.

It was really odd having two strangers there watching us while we chatted. It was lovely to see Jimmy, and I longed to run over and cuddle him and cover him with kisses but I was worried about what the key workers might think. In the end, when he saw me he crawled straight over to me.

'Oh, look, he's crawling,' I said. 'Clever boy.'

'Yeah, he started the other day,' said Jess proudly.

She and Darren were very quiet and the conversation felt very forced and stilted with the two strangers there.

'Are you sure you're OK?' I asked them. 'Are you settling in all right?'

'Fine,' said Jess.

It was all very strange.

'I think I'll put the kettle on,' I said, in a desperate attempt to give me something to do.

'Would you like a cup of tea?' I asked the key workers, but they looked surprised that someone had talked to them. They both shook their heads.

'No thanks,' one of them said.

Lily came over to me in the kitchen while I was making the tea.

'Who are them ladies, and why are they just staring at us?' she asked.

Everyone looked really embarrassed.

'They work here, darling, and they're just making sure that Jess and Darren are happy and Jimmy is OK,' I told her.

We stayed for two hours, and by the end of it I was exhausted after trying to keep the conversation going. I could see Lily was getting restless, so we made our excuses and left.

On the way out I popped in to see Hannah, the centre manager.

'When I come and visit next time, I just wondered whether I would be allowed to take Jess, Darren and Jimmy out?' I asked. 'I thought it would be nice to go for a meal and give them a bit of breathing space.'

'I don't think that would be possible, unfortunately,' she said. 'We can only let someone else out with Jimmy if they're police-checked and they're willing to take responsibility for him.'

'I am police-checked,' I said. 'I'm a foster carer.'

'Oh, yes, of course,' she said. 'Well in that case, that should be fine. We'd need you to text us every hour to let us know Jimmy is OK, and you'd have to make sure Jess and Darren were never left alone with him.'

'That's absolutely fine,' I said.

On the drive back, the girls were both very quiet.

'That place was weird,' said Louisa. 'I couldn't stand having someone watching me like that all the time.'

'If you had to do that in order to keep your baby I suspect you'd stick it out,' I said.

'I liked their new flat,' said Lily. 'But I didn't like those grumpy ladies.'

In the two weeks leading up to our next visit I got the odd text from Jess.

Yippee we're down to one key worker watching us!! she wrote.

Well done that's brilliant, I replied.

I drove down there one Saturday to visit them. Lily was staying with her mum for the weekend so I just brought Louisa.

'Get your coats on,' I told them when we went up to the flat. 'I'm taking you out for lunch.'

'What?' gasped Jess. 'Are you joking?'

'We ain't allowed to go out on our own with Jimmy,' said Darren.

'You're not on your own,' I said. 'You're with me, and your manager's agreed that's fine as long as Jimmy is in my sight all the time.'

214

'That's amazing,' said Jess.

They couldn't wait to get out of there, and it was clearly a relief for them to be away from the assessment centre. I could physically see Jess's shoulders drop as she got into the car and she gave a massive sigh. It took another hour or so before they both fully relaxed.

'I don't mind you watching us – it just starts getting to you in there after a while,' said Darren.

'It's so nice to chat without feeling like someone's checking up on you all the time,' sighed Jess. 'I didn't know it would be so hard.'

'How do you think it's going?' I asked them as we tucked into lunch at a pub we'd found in a nearby village.

'OK,' sighed Darren. 'We're trying really hard, but we keep doing stuff wrong.'

Jess explained how they'd been given verbal warnings about not keeping the flat clean and tidy, not washing clothes and bedding frequently enough and forgetting to wash her hands before she made Jimmy's bottle.

'I'm so worried that we're going to fail that I'm stressed out of my head,' she said.

'When they told you all these things, did you remember to do them the next time?' I asked.

Jess nodded.

'Well then, you're fine,' I said. 'You've shown them that you've listened to their concerns, and when you've had something pointed out to you you've made sure that you've changed it. That's all you can do.'

'We're trying so, so hard,' she said.

'I know you are, love,' I told her.

It felt strange that when Jimmy needed his nappy changing I had to go with Jess and watch her do it. For the past seven months I'd been doing all I could to encourage Jess and Darren to care for their son and be hands-on, and now it felt like we'd taken a step back.

I could see they were both reluctant to go back to the centre.

'I really don't want to go in there,' groaned Jess as we pulled up outside.

To my surprise, it was Darren who gave her a pep talk.

'It's what we have to do to get Jimmy back, so we've got to get on with it,' he told her. 'We're doing all right. We're good parents, Jess.'

'I know, Daz,' she sighed. 'It's just so hard.'

Little did we know things were about to get much harder, and their dedication was really going to be put to the test.

SIXTEEN

An Emergency Dash

For once, it was an oasis of calm at my house. A chicken casserole was bubbling away in the oven, Louisa was in the bath and I was helping Lily do her homework. Then Jess rang.

She'd been at the assessment centre for five weeks and things, on the face of it, seemed to be going well.

'Hi, sweetie, are you OK?' I asked.

Immediately from the tone of her voice I could tell that she wasn't.

'Maggie, it's all gone wrong,' she said, her voice taut and breathless.

'Oh, no,' I gasped, my heart sinking at the thought of what she was about to tell me. 'What's happened?'

She hardly paused for breath as she launched into her story.

'I felt really poorly today so when Jimmy had a nap, I lay down on the bed too,' she said. 'I fell asleep but I was supposed to be at group therapy downstairs and the key worker came up and got me and she was really cross.

'Now they're saying I'm not committed and I got really upset and started crying, and Daz and I had an argument because he said I should have told them I was poorly.'

My brain was whirring, trying to take it all in.

'Well, *did* you tell them that you weren't well?' I asked.

'When the key worker came and got me I said I was sick, but I didn't have a chance to before cos I'd fallen asleep,' she said. 'And now I'm worried cos Darren and I were shouting at each other and they might think we're bad parents.'

'Take a deep breath and calm down, Jess,' I told her. 'It's OK to be ill, but if you can't make a session, you need to let people know. As long as they know, it doesn't matter. Communication is the key. So you need to apologise and promise them that you won't do it again.'

'I have,' she said.

'And as for you and Darren, all couples have arguments,' I said. 'Where was Jimmy when you were arguing?'

'He was still asleep in the bedroom,' she said.

'Well, there you go,' I told her. 'You weren't arguing in front of him and he wasn't frightened or distressed. What did they say was going to happen to you?'

'I got a written warning,' she said. 'That's really bad, innit?'

'It's your first one, and it's not the end of the world,' I said. 'It will be recorded in your notes, but as long as you show that you've taken what they've said on board, learnt from it and don't do it again then you should be absolutely fine.'

Jess had wound herself up into a frenzy and needed reassurance. I think all the stress and strain of living at the assessment centre was coming to a head and the cracks were starting to show.

'Remember what I told you when you first came to live with

me?' I said. 'You can't do everything right. Nobody's perfect. Not even me.'

At least that made her laugh.

'How's everything else?' I asked.

'OK, I suppose,' she said. 'Daz has taken really well to the therapy although I don't like it. I think all that talking's pointless and I'm worried they're gonna use it against me.'

'What kinds of things have they encouraged you to talk about?' I asked.

'My dad, but I said I ain't never even seen him. I told them my mum said he wanted nothing to do with me. I don't even know who he is, so how can I talk about him?'

'What about your mum?' I asked.

'Yeah, they tried to get me to say how I felt about her. All I said was I'm never going to be like she was with Jimmy. I'm going to be there for him and cook his tea and give him cuddles. All I got was swore at and told to go to my room cos she had a man coming round.'

'It can't all be bad there,' I said. 'Is there anything that you're enjoying?'

'I like it when we have a meal together with the other families and we can chat,' she said. 'Daz is getting on really well with the bloke in the flat next door. Him and his wife are in here with their three kids.'

'Do you know why they're being assessed?' I asked.

'It's loads worse than me and Daz,' she said. 'They were drinkers and he went to prison, but now they're both clean and getting their act together.'

'It's good that you're making friends,' I said. 'You take care of yourselves. Try and stay calm, and I'll see you soon.'

All I could hope was that Jess wouldn't let the pressure get to her. A week later, the girls and I went down to visit. I was confused to see two key workers sitting in the flat.

'I thought you were down to one person watching you?' I said to Jess when we went to make a cup of tea in the kitchen.

'Ask Darren about that,' she sighed.

He was very sheepish as he told me how he had gone round to see his friend Phil in the flat next door and had stayed until 11 p.m. when a worker had found him there.

'The rules are you're not allowed to visit another flat after 9 p.m.,' said Jess. 'I told Daz that. The key worker gave him a verbal warning and then the bloody idiot went and did it again.'

'What happened?' I asked him.

'I had to go down to the office and have a talk with the manager and I got a written warning,' he said. 'They've said we've got to have two workers again for another week until I prove I can be trusted.'

I was really disappointed in him as he was ruining all the good work they'd done in the first few weeks.

'Darren, I can't believe you've been so irresponsible,' I said. 'Is it really worth risking losing your son just so you can sit around at your mate's house?

'Were you drinking?' I asked.

'No, we wasn't,' he said. 'There's no way we'd do that. Phil would be kicked out, as he used to be an alky. We was just chatting and playing on his Xbox and I didn't know what time it was.'

I was annoyed that his stupidity had resulted in a written warning.

'Seriously, Darren, you need to get your act together,' I said. 'Another warning and you could be asked to leave. Is that fair on Jess? You're meant to be working as a team here, and supporting each other.'

Understandably, Jess was furious with him.

'It couldn't be worse timing,' she said. 'We've got that meeting next week and I'm worried sick they're going to chuck us out.'

Six weeks into the assessment they were due to have their midpoint review to discuss how things were going. Debbie would be going down to the centre as well as Kimberly, the IRO. I knew Jess was incredibly nervous about it, especially after the wobbles they'd had over the past couple of weeks.

'You'll be absolutely fine,' I told her. 'Ring me afterwards if you want to have a chat.'

Debbie wasn't obliged to keep me in the loop any more because Jimmy was no longer in my care, so technically I wasn't involved in the case and it was confidential information. However, that didn't mean I wasn't emotionally involved.

On the day of the meeting I was on tenterhooks all morning, so I was relieved when Jess rang.

'Well?' I asked.

'You was right,' she told me. 'They all said it was going really well and the signs were positive. We don't have to have twenty-four-hour supervision any more, just people in the daytime.'

'That's brilliant,' I told her. 'You must be so pleased.'

'It will be nice not to have people watching us all the time and be able to pick Jimmy up out of his cot when he cries without checking with someone else,' she said.

I hoped it was the boost they both needed to get through the last few weeks of the assessment.

'Louisa and I will be down next weekend for Darren's birthday,' I said. 'So we'll see you then.'

'Where's Lily?' she asked.

'She's going to her mum's so she can't come, I'm afraid,' I said.

Lily must have heard me talking on the phone.

'Why can't I come to Darren's party?' she asked when I hung up.

'It's your weekend with Mummy,' I said.

'Can you ask her if I can come?' she begged. 'Please. I want to see Darren.'

'I'll see what I can do,' I promised.

I phoned Jane and explained, and she was happy for us to come and pick Lily up and take her to the assessment centre for the afternoon.

'How are things going?' I asked her.

'Brilliantly,' she said. 'Lily seems to be enjoying spending time here, and we've talked about getting her a kitten when she comes to live with me.'

'Yes, she told me,' I said. 'She told me all about her room, and the little girl who lives next door who she was playing with.'

'Thanks for letting her come with us at the weekend. It's Darren's eighteenth, so it's a bit of a special celebration for him.'

I thought it was important to acknowledge his birthday even though he hadn't mentioned it. The girls and I baked him a cake and made him some cards and we bought him some socks, a mug and a *Now That's What I Call Music* CD.

Jess let us into the flat while he was downstairs in the playroom with Jimmy and we decorated the living room with balloons and banners. When he came back up, we were all waiting.

'Surprise!' we yelled.

He looked chuffed as well as a little bit embarrassed.

'Nobody's ever made a fuss of me like this,' he said. 'I've never even got a card from me mum.'

I'd given Jess a special kit so she could do Jimmy's foot- and handprints in paint and make them into a card for Darren and he was really touched by that.

I drove home later that day with a smile on my face. Things were going well for them at last, as well as for Lily too. Fingers crossed that everyone was going to get their happy ending.

But of course nothing ever runs smoothly, and a few nights later I got a phone call in the early hours of the morning. It was Jess, and she sounded hysterical. My first thought was that Darren had done something stupid again, so I wasn't expecting what she said next.

'It's Jimmy,' she said. 'He's been rushed to hospital.'

'What?' I gasped. 'Is he OK?'

'I don't know,' she sobbed. 'He's attached to loads of wires and machines and they're doing tests. Oh, Maggie, I'm so scared he's going to die.'

'Slow down and tell me what happened,' I said.

Jess explained that Jimmy had been in the playroom and that one of the workers thought he'd felt a bit hot, so she'd taken him up to the flat and given him some Calpol. The next day he was off his food and still had a temperature, so she and a key worker had taken him to see the GP.

'He said it was a virus and to keep giving him Calpol to reduce his temperature,' she said.

But late last night he'd taken a turn for the worse.

'He'd been sleeping all day and when I tried to wake him up for his bottle he was all floppy and he wasn't breathing properly,' she sobbed. 'Then I saw the rash.'

'Oh, Jess,' I said. 'You poor thing.'

It must have been terrifying for them. The centre had called an ambulance and Jimmy had been blue-lighted to the local hospital.

'Do the doctors know what it might be?' I asked.

'They don't know, but they're worried it's something called meningitis. That's serious, ain't it, Maggie?'

My heart sank. Meningitis was every parent's worst nightmare – I couldn't lie to her.

'Yes,' I said. 'I'm afraid it can be very serious.'

'I'm so scared that we've blown it and the centre are going to stop the assessment,' she wept. 'We're so close to the end, but now this has happened and they're going to think it's all my fault. I must be a bad mum if my baby's ended up in hospital.'

'Don't be silly, this is nothing to do with you,' I said. 'You did the right thing. You took Jimmy to see the doctor.

'You couldn't have done any more. You shouldn't even be thinking about the assessment now.'

But Jess refused to believe that this wasn't her fault.

'I'll be there as soon as I can,' I told her. 'I'll drop Lily off at school and drive straight to the hospital.'

'Thank you,' she said. 'Daz and I would like that.'

By the time I put the phone down, it had started to get light. It was a lovely sunny June morning, and I sat at the kitchen table with a cup of tea and looked out at the garden.

Please let Jimmy be OK, I thought.

I knew how serious meningitis could be – in fact, a friend of mine had fostered a little boy once who had lost an arm and a leg to the disease and he'd been lucky to survive. No parent deserved that, especially not after everything Jess and Darren had been through. They couldn't lose their son now after fighting to be with him for so long. It was unthinkable.

I waited until 8 a.m. before I phoned Debbie.

'I'm assuming you know about Jimmy?' I said. 'Would it be OK if I went to see them at the hospital?'

'Of course,' she told me. 'The assessment centre called me late last night when they went to hospital. They need all the support they can get right now.'

I also mentioned Jess's fears to her.

'She's worried that somehow Jimmy being in hospital will reflect badly on her and Darren. I've tried to reassure her, but it's just adding to her stress.'

'Poor kid,' sighed Debbie. 'I'll have a chat to her about it the next time I speak to her.

'Maggie, will you give me a call and let me know how Jimmy is?'

'Of course,' I said.

Later that morning I arrived at the hospital and was directed to the children's ward. I found Jess and Darren sitting in the reception area. They looked like two frightened kids.

I went over to them and Jess threw her arms around me.

'How is he?' I asked.

'The doctors are doing tests,' Darren sighed.

'They had to take fluid out of his spine and it was horrible,' said Jess. 'They were holding him down and he was crying. I had to go out, I couldn't bear it.'

I got them both a can of Coke out of a vending machine as they didn't have any money on them, and we all sat in the waiting area.

'I'm so scared, Maggie,' said Jess. 'We've fought so hard to keep Jimmy and now he might die.'

'It's going to be OK,' I told her, stroking her hair. 'The doctors are doing all they can and hopefully they caught it early.'

She sobbed in my arms.

'Do you think I could see him?' I asked.

Jess nodded. Jimmy was in an isolation room. He was nine months old now, and he looked so tiny and helpless lying there in a big bed. He was attached to a drip and was only wearing a nappy so I could see the mottled red rash on his podgy little tummy.

I held back the tears. I knew I needed to keep it together for Jess's sake. I had to stay strong for her.

'Hello, little man,' I said, stroking his fluffy brown hair. 'You've got your mummy and daddy very worried, you know.'

All we could do was watch and wait.

I went outside and phoned Debbie.

'The doctors are still doing tests but he's stable,' I said.

'Keep in touch,' she told me.

I spent the rest of the day at the hospital with Jess and Darren, pacing the corridors, sitting on uncomfortable chairs and making multiple trips to the canteen for cups of tea. I tried to persuade the pair of them to eat, but neither of them would touch a mouthful. Eventually a consultant came out to see them.

Jess grabbed Darren's hand and I could see she was steeling herself for bad news.

'The results have come back and I'm pleased to say that it's not meningitis,' she said. 'It's a virus, so we're getting some fluids into him to keep him hydrated and to keep his temperature down and we're starting him on some strong antibiotics. He'll probably have to stay in another night, but he's going to be fine.'

Darren smiled. Jess burst into tears.

'I don't believe it,' she said. 'Thank God.'

I took them to the canteen for a cup of tea and managed to persuade them to eat some chips.

'You should go home, Maggie,' said Jess. 'What about Lily?'

'Don't worry – her mum is picking her up from school today, so she's fine.'

'Honestly, go home and get some rest. Me and Daz will be fine.'

'Make sure you ring me if you need anything,' I said. 'And don't worry about the assessment centre. Just concentrate on Jimmy getting better.'

'I will,' she said.

Thankfully, Jimmy turned a corner. A couple of days later he was discharged from hospital and we all breathed a sigh of relief.

They were nine weeks into their assessment now and only had three weeks left. Finally the end was in sight, but as it drew closer, Jess got more and more anxious.

'I really hope we pass,' she said. 'I can't sleep at night worrying about it.'

'It's not about pass or fail,' I tried to explain to her. 'Yes, it's an assessment, but the very fact that you're still here means that you are passing.'

The crucial point was the ten-week transitional meeting. This was where everyone got together to decide what was going to happen next and where Darren, Jess and Jimmy would go at the end of the assessment period. This was where it was decided whether plans would be put in place for them all to live together, or whether Social Services would apply for a permanent care order for Jimmy and adoption proceedings would be started.

I did my best to reassure Jess, but we all knew how important this was. Whatever was decided at this meeting was going to affect the rest of their lives. They'd been fighting for ten months to be a family and keep their baby, and now they were about to be told whether or not this could happen.

The morning of the meeting, I did my best to take my mind off it and keep busy. I decided to start sorting through Lily's bedroom and begin to pack up her things ahead of her permanent move to her mum's. But even that mammoth task didn't distract me, and I felt sick with nerves.

They'll be fine, I told myself. They had to be.

The very fact that they were still at the centre proved that everything had gone OK. However, I also knew that these assessments had very strict criteria and they could be extended by up to six months if anyone had any niggle of doubt about Jess and Darren's parenting. I wasn't sure if they'd be able to cope with another three months there.

Just after lunch my mobile rang and I jumped on it.

'Jess,' I gasped. 'What happened?'

'We've had the meeting and they told us they've made a decision,' she said.

I couldn't tell by the tone of her voice whether it was good or bad news.

'And what did they say?' I asked, desperate to know the outcome. 'Tell me Jess, please.'

SEVENTEEN

The Right Move

The suspense was killing me.

'Go on, then,' I said. 'Put me out of my misery. What happened?'

'We've done it!' she shrieked down the phone. 'Jimmy is ours! We can keep him, Maggie. I'm so, so happy.'

'Jess, he's always been yours,' I laughed, my heart swelling with pride. 'Tell me exactly what they said to you.'

'We had the meeting and they said that they don't have any concerns about me and Daz as parents, and there was no reason why Jimmy couldn't live with us permanently.'

'That is brilliant,' I said. 'I'm so proud of you both. How do you feel?'

'I've been crying all morning cos I was so worried they were going to take him away and I'm still crying, but now they're happy tears,' she said. 'It's what we wanted all along. I honestly can't believe it's happened.'

She sounded euphoric.

'Well, you should believe it,' I told her. 'You and Darren are good parents. I know that, the assessment centre knows that and now so do Social Services. All three of you can be a family at last. What does Daz think?'

'Oh, he's well chuffed. Don't tell him I told you, Maggie, but he had a bit of a blub too.'

They had to stay at the centre for the last couple of weeks but they would be able to live independently. That meant they could go in and out as they pleased, only attend therapy or play sessions if they wanted and they didn't have to have any supervision.

'It must feel good that the pressure's off and you're not being observed any more,' I said.

'To be honest, Maggie, I can't wait to get out of here,' she replied.

Jess explained that because they were leaving the assessment centre, they were top of the council housing list.

'I hope we get a place near you,' she said.

'You'll have to take whatever comes up,' I told her. 'Some people have to wait months for a council house, so you're incredibly lucky.'

As soon as I put the phone down to Jess, Debbie rang.

'I'm sure Jess has already told you but the good news is we won't be needing you to take Jimmy back,' she said. 'He'll be staying with Jess and Darren.

'We won't be proceeding with the care order, and we'll be withdrawing the ICO.'

'I heard,' I said. 'I'm so pleased for them, and bloomin' relieved too.'

'To be honest, Maggie, a few months ago when I first took over this case I never, ever thought that this would be the outcome,' she told me. 'I didn't think they were mature enough to cope with being responsible parents and I thought they'd crack under the pressure of the assessment centre.

'But they've proved us all wrong. It's lucky they had you fighting for them.'

'I always believed that, despite their age, with the right help and support they could do this,' I said.

I felt so proud that my actions had helped keep this little family together. I also felt vindicated and slightly relieved – I'd taken a real leap of faith when I'd put my professional reputation on the line and spoken up in defence of Jess and Darren and their ability to be good parents, when everyone else was in favour of adoption. There are not many happy endings in fostering, and it was wonderful moments like this that made doing my job so worthwhile.

It didn't mean the end of all Social Services' involvement. Jess and Darren had agreed that a worker from the family centre could come and see them once a week and check that they were all OK and coping with living on their own.

I couldn't wait to see Jess and Darren and give them a big hug, so I visited them a few days later. They were still on cloud nine. It was like a weight had been lifted from their shoulders and they looked so happy.

'Daz has been applying for jobs,' Jess told me proudly.

'That's great,' I said.

He explained how the staff had been helping him fill in application forms and do practice interviews.

'What sort of thing are you going for?' I asked.

'Anything, really,' he said. 'Labouring on a building site or working at a supermarket. I'm not fussy.'

Jess told me how a council flat had just come up about fifteen minutes away from me.

'Will you come and look at it with us, Maggie?' she asked.

'If you want me to then of course I will,' I replied.

We went round to see it a couple of days later. It was a two-bed ground floor flat with a little garden. The kitchen and bathroom were very old-fashioned and well worn but it was clean and the walls had been newly painted.

'It's great.' Jess grinned. 'I love it.'

'I can't believe it's all ours and no one's going to be coming in to check up on us,' said Darren.

'Yes – you're on your own now.' I smiled.

It was unfurnished, so the rooms were empty and bare.

'But there's not any carpet down,' said Jess. 'Jimmy can't crawl around on that hard floor.'

'What are we gonna do?' asked Darren. 'We can't afford to buy no furniture.'

'The centre will talk to you about it, but through income support you'll be entitled to something called a home start grant,' I said. 'That will enable you to buy all the basics, so don't worry.'

The grant covered essential items like a bed, a sofa, a table, a cooker and some crockery and pans.

'I've got some things for Jimmy you can have,' I told them. 'You can have my cot and Jimmy's mattress, because I have to get a new one for each child, and you can have my buggy and the spare high chair from the loft.

'When I next come down I'll take you shopping and we can get a few more bits and pieces.'

'Ta, Maggie,' said Jess. 'I don't know what we'd do without you.'

I wanted to make sure they had a proper understanding of bills, so I had a look in one of the cupboards and found the gas and electricity meter.

'It's a card meter,' I said. 'So that's easy to manage.'

Jess looked at me blankly.

'You need to make sure you keep the card topped up and then you'll soon work out how much gas and electric you use and how much you need to budget for,' I explained.

'Oh, I see,' she said. 'Yeah, one of the workers mentioned something about a card.'

She sounded a bit vague, but I had faith that they could cope with running a home on their own. For the past three months, they'd been taught how to stick to a budget and pay household bills. They could do a supermarket shop and make basic meals like mince and potatoes and fish fingers, chips and beans.

Debbie had spoken to them about letting their mums know where they were.

'She asked me if I wanted to get in touch with my mum and tell her about the flat but I said no way,' Jess told me. 'She didn't want nothing to do with us before, and she never came to visit us in the family centre. She couldn't care less, so why should we tell her where we've moved to?'

She and Darren had disagreed about whether to let his mum know or not.

'I'd like my mum to know we've moved and got our own place,' said Darren.

'Why?' said Jess. 'They ain't bothered with us since we went to the family centre. I don't want your brothers coming round here and ruining it all. What do you think, Maggie?'

'It's not my decision to make,' I said. 'We can't choose our family and we can't change them, but it might be nice to let Darren's mum know you've got your own flat.

'If you don't give her the address then no one can just turn up, but they've got your number so they can ring you if they want to see you.'

'I don't want them in our lives no more,' sighed Jess. 'We can't risk it, Daz. What if you get dragged into trouble and the police get involved? If that happens then Social Services will be round here. We can't risk it.'

Jess was determined nothing was going to jeopardise her little family that she'd fought so hard for, and I didn't blame her. I was so proud of her.

On my next visit to the assessment centre, I took Jess and Darren out shopping. I bought them a few little household things they didn't know that they'd need like a washing-up bowl, an airer to dry their clothes on, some pans and a kitchen bin.

'While we're here, Darren, let's get you a shirt and tie so you've got something to wear for job interviews,' I suggested.

'I'm only applying to Tesco and Aldi,' he said. 'I'll just wear a T-shirt.'

'Darren, there's so much competition for jobs these days, and if you turn up in a scruffy T-shirt or sweatshirt it speaks volumes. No matter what the job, it's important for you to look clean and smart.'

'OK,' he sighed.

'Daz, do you want a job or not?' said Jess.

'I do,' he said. 'I just think it's a bit over the top.'

Again I rallied my foster carer troops together and they all came up with things to help furnish Jess and Darren's flat. Anne and Bob had a pair of curtains they didn't want any more and Vicky had a rug and some cushions they could have.

A week later, they were due to move out of the centre. Staff there had a van to take them and their things to the new flat, although to be honest they didn't have much. I went to collect

Jimmy and took him back to my house for the day while they got unpacked and sorted.

'I'll drop Jimmy back at the flat later,' I told them. 'I can't wait to see it.'

I'd got a few things ready to bring them like a bunch of flowers in a vase because I knew they didn't have one, and a cardboard box of kitchen essentials like salt and pepper, oil, jam, tins of beans, tea bags, bread, milk, washing-up liquid and loo rolls to get them started. I'd also got them some cupboard locks and plug socket covers to make sure everything was safe for Jimmy.

'Maggie, you're the best,' said Jess, flinging her arms around me. 'You get us stuff we don't even know we need until you bring it.'

A new carpet had been put down since we'd looked around, a cooker had been fitted and the furniture had arrived, although it was all still wrapped in plastic.

'I don't know where to start,' sighed Darren.

'Unfortunately I'm not known for my DIY skills,' I said. 'Tell you what. I'll give Anne's husband Bob a ring, he's very handy. Maybe he could nip round later and at least help you get the bed set up?'

Bob was happy to answer my cry for help and both he and Anne came round. Anne helped Jess and I put up some curtains while Bob and Darren tackled their bed and Jimmy's cot.

By 9 p.m. that night the place was still looking very bare but at least they had somewhere to sleep. Jess put Jimmy to bed while I made us all a cup of tea and we stood out in the little courtyard garden. It was a lovely summer's evening, and Jess and Darren were exhausted but happy.

'Here's wishing you lots of happiness in your new home,' I said, and we all did 'cheers' with our mugs.

Jess and Darren were like two excited kids on Christmas Eve, and they couldn't wait to spend their first night in their new home as a family.

'I think we're gonna be really happy here.' Jess smiled.

'When you're settled in you'll have to see if there are any playgroups on the estate that you can take Jimmy to,' I suggested.

Jess shook her head.

'Don't fancy it,' she sighed. 'I bet all the other mums will be much older and will turn their noses up at me.'

'It's good to get yourselves out and about,' I told her.

It was after 10 p.m. before I left, and I was shattered.

'You'll have to bring Lily and Louisa next time you come,' said Jess as I was leaving.

'I can bring Louisa, but Lily's going to be moving back in with her mum next week,' I said.

'Blimey, everyone's moving,' laughed Darren.

It was true. We were in the last week of the handover, and I was in denial about the fact that Lily was really going. All the excitement of Jess and Darren being allowed to keep Jimmy had taken my mind off what was about to happen at home.

'I bet you'll miss her,' said Jess.

That was an understatement. Like Jimmy, Lily was one of those children who had stolen my heart. After living with me for four years she was like a daughter to me, and I knew that losing her was going to feel like a bereavement. As I drove home that night, my heart was heavy as I realised there was no putting it off any longer. In a few days' time I'd have to say goodbye to Lily.

EIGHTEEN

Goodbye Again

As we walked through the department store, Lily's eyes were as wide as saucers.

'Look at that glittery vase,' she gasped. 'Can I get them that?'

She desperately wanted to buy Jess and Darren a present for their new flat and I'd promised to take her shopping before she left.

'What about this?' I said, pointing to a jewelled photo frame.

'It's lovely,' she sighed. 'I'd like that. Can I have it for my bedroom?'

'You're going to be at your mummy's,' I said. 'But how about I get it you for your new bedroom at Mummy's house?'

Lily's face lit up.

'Ooh yes, I would love that,' she said. 'I bet Mummy would like it too. I could put a photo of you and Louisa in it.'

'That's a great idea.' I smiled.

We were at the till paying for it when I felt Lily's little hand entwine with mine. I gave it a squeeze and quickly blinked back the tears in my eyes so she wouldn't see them.

'I'll miss you, Maggie, when I go,' she said sadly. 'And Louisa too.'

'You won't have time to miss us,' I told her, doing my best to be upbeat even though inside I felt like sobbing. 'You're coming round next week for your tea.'

I was going to miss her so, so much, but I knew it would only upset Lily to see me weeping and wailing. I wanted to make going to live with her mum a positive thing and I didn't want her to feel guilty about leaving us.

It was the final couple of days before Lily left to go and live with her mum. We'd got to the point where she was spending most of the time at Jane's anyway. She'd chosen the toys she wanted to take with her, and each day I'd sent over some more of her things. She had four years' worth of stuff, so there was a lot to move.

Although my heart was breaking at the thought of her going to live with her mum, she was so excited about it. Despite my upset, I was genuinely thrilled for her. None of us had seen it coming, but as a foster carer my main priority is to keep families together wherever possible, and it was lovely that she was going back to be with her biological mum. The plan to move her over couldn't have gone any smoother, either. As it had been so gradual, we'd all had time to get used to it.

After we'd finished our shopping, I took Lily for a milkshake. 'So are you excited about going to live at Mummy's?' I asked her. She nodded.

'I'm glad Daddy's not going to be there,' she said, fiddling with her straw. 'I haven't seen him since I was a very little girl.'

It was the first time in a long while that she'd mentioned her dad. When she'd first been taken into care, he was offered supervised contact but had failed to turn up to any of the sessions and it was cancelled. Social Services hadn't heard from him since then.

'What do you remember about Daddy?' I asked her.

'He always smelt a bit funny,' she said. 'You know like when we go round to Vicky's or Anne's house at Christmas and the grown-ups are drinking them drinks out of bottles and cans.'

'You mean beer and wine?' I said, and Lily nodded.

'Yeah, like that,' she replied. 'But I didn't like it.

'And I didn't like it when he was being silly one day and he picked me up but his legs went all wobbly and he dropped me. I hurt my head and it was really sore. And he was mean to Mummy too. I remember that.

'I don't really want to see Daddy,' she told me, slurping her milkshake.

'You won't have to,' I said. 'It's just going to be you and Mummy, I promise.'

Thankfully Lily seemed reassured.

On the Friday afternoon before she left, we had a little party after school. Vicky and Anne and their foster children came round and I did a buffet tea – just like we'd done for Jimmy. Lily was excited, running around with the other children, opening her 'good luck in your new home' cards and the little pressies everyone had bought her.

'How are you feeling about it all?' Anne asked me. 'You've been saying a lot of goodbyes recently.'

I shrugged my shoulders sadly.

'It never gets any easier, does it?' I sighed. 'I'm finding this one really hard.'

'It's understandable,' she said. 'She's been with you for so long, she's part of your family. Be kind to yourself and give yourself a chance to grieve.'

'I will,' I said.

Grieving was exactly what it was. I was grieving at having to say goodbye to a child who I thought was going to be with me long-term, and for the fact that there was going to be someone missing in our family.

When everyone had gone, Louisa and I gave Lily our present. She looked puzzled when I handed her a small box.

'It's tiny,' she said.

'Trust me, all the best stuff comes in small boxes,' Louisa told her.

She gasped when she saw the little silver star necklace inside.

'It's a star,' I told her. 'Because you're our little star.'

'I love it,' she said. 'Can I wear it now?'

'OK,' I laughed.

As she grinned at me I realised how much I'd miss that little freckled face and her gappy smile with the front two teeth missing.

Later that night I tucked her in for the last time. I knew she was happy about going to live with her mum, but suddenly all the worries that she had been saving up in her head came tumbling out.

'Will you miss me, Maggie?' she asked.

'Of course I will, but I'm going to see you next week when you come round,' I told her.

'Will other children be coming to live in your house and sleep in this bedroom?'

'Yes, they will, lovely. Just like other children slept in it a long time ago before you came. I don't know who they are yet, though.'

'Do you think you and Louisa will forget me when the other children come?' she asked.

'No, because we'll still see you,' I told her. 'And besides, how could I forget someone who always leaves their wet towels on the bathroom floor and their felt tips all over my kitchen table? I could never forget someone as messy as you,' I joked.

'Now you get to sleep,' I said, kissing her forehead. 'The only thing that's changing is where you're sleeping. You're staying at the same school, so you'll have the same teacher and the same friends. And you'll still see me and Louisa. We're not going anywhere.'

But the questions kept coming.

'Are you glad I'm going to live with Mummy?'

'I'm glad for Mummy, and I'm glad that you're going home because that's what you want, and I will miss you lots and lots.

'Now goodnight,' I said, getting up and walking out.

'Maggie?' Lily called out. 'Will you still keep my photo in that frame on your dresser when I've gone?'

'Yes, of course I will,' I said. 'Your photo will always stay on my dresser for ever and ever. Now, sleepy time. You've got an exciting day tomorrow.'

As I went downstairs I hoped I'd done my best to reassure her.

I didn't sleep much that night. I tossed and turned and worried about whether Lily was OK. In the morning I went into her bedroom to get the last few things to take to her mum's house. I stripped her bed so that she could take her sheets with her, and there were a couple of books she'd been reading. As I looked around her bedroom, it all seemed so bare. There was nothing left on the walls except the odd Blu-Tack mark where her drawings and certificates from school and swimming had been stuck up. They were all in her memory box now, which was another thing that she had to take with her. I had a last quick look through it before I put the lid on. She'd chosen some photos to take with her and I'd put them in an album, and there were little souvenirs from holidays that we'd been on over the years and even an old ring box with some of her baby teeth in it. Right at the bottom was an old stuffed toy dog.

'What's that?' asked Lily, coming in.

'It's Digby,' I said. 'When you first came here you took him everywhere with you.

'He was really grubby. He used to get bits of food on him as you'd insist on putting him next to your plate when you had dinner and once you even dropped him down the toilet. I had to sneak him away and wash him when you were at nursery.'

Lily grinned.

'Oh yeah, I think I remember,' she said. 'I don't have Digby now, though – I'm a big girl.'

'No,' I told her. 'But it would be nice for you to take him to Mummy's and he will help you remember being here.'

'I'll always remember being here,' she said. 'I'm going downstairs now, to see Louisa.'

'OK,' I said.

I looked down at the stuffed dog in my hands and remembered the frightened little four-year-old who had first come to live with me. She'd been taken into care suddenly after seeing her mum being beaten up by her dad. I also remembered the terrible temper tantrums that had followed, and struggling to find a nursery that would take this angry girl who destroyed toys and overturned tables. Worlds away from the polite, kind, seven-year-old girl we were saying goodbye to today.

For the past couple of days it had taken all my energy and strength to hide my upset from the girls and keep things upbeat.

I couldn't do it any longer.

'I'm just going for a quick shower,' I shouted down to the living room where Louisa was helping Lily pack the last of her toys.

I shut the bathroom door, turned the shower on, sat down on the closed toilet seat and sobbed my heart out, safe in the knowledge that neither of them could hear me. I felt the loss of Lily like a physical pain.

After I'd got myself together, I got dressed and we all piled into the car.

'It's time to go to Mummy's.' Lily smiled.

Jane's terrace was only a short drive from our house. As we pulled up outside, she was already standing at the front door waving and smiling.

'Come and see my new bedroom,' Lily told us.

'Is that OK?' I asked Jane.

'Of course,' she said. 'Come in.'

It was a nice homely house, and it was lovely to see Lily's things scattered around already. Her drawings were on the kitchen wall, there were photos of her stuck on the fridge and there were pots of pens and crayons and piles of puzzle books and drawing pads around – all things that I knew Lily loved to do.

Lily proudly showed us her new bedroom. I noticed that she'd lined her soft toys up in exactly the same way they'd been at my house, like she was trying to create a replica of her old bedroom.

'It's lovely,' I said. 'I bet you sleep really well in here.'

I always like to keep goodbyes brief, and thanks to Louisa's impatience, that was exactly what happened.

'Can we go now?' she whispered. 'You said we could go shopping, and I really want to go to Lush.'

To cheer us both up after dropping Lily off, I'd planned lunch and a girly shopping trip to town.

'I'm afraid we'd better be going now,' I told Jane.

I gave Lily a big hug.

'I'm going to miss you lots,' I said. 'But I'll see you next week when you come round.'

'Bye.' She waved, completely nonchalant.

'Can I watch telly now, Mummy?' she asked.

We'd dropped her off and picked her up so many times from her mum's house over the past few months when she'd come to stay, so in a way this didn't feel any different to her.

'Thank you for everything, Maggie,' said Jane as we walked outside towards the car.

I couldn't catch her eye otherwise I knew I'd burst into tears, and I didn't think it was appropriate for Jane to see me upset. Instead, I rummaged through my handbag with trembling hands, pretending to look for my car keys. I took a few deep breaths and managed to make it to the car without breaking down. I gave her a cheerful wave goodbye as we drove away.

*

That was that. It was done, and Lily was gone. Even though I felt like collapsing in a sobbing heap, I had to stay strong for Louisa. I didn't want her to be upset.

'How do you feel about Lily going?' I asked her as we drove into town.

'It doesn't really feel real yet,' she said. 'It just like she's gone to her mum's for the weekend.'

'I know what you mean,' I said.

I knew it would take a while for it to hit us both. We had a nice day together, and on the way home I dropped Louisa off at her friend's house where she was staying the night.

As I walked through the front door at home, I had a funny feeling. I realised that for the first time literally in years I had an entire night on my own in the house. It felt very odd and eerily quiet. It was a lovely summer's night, and even though it was still warm, I wanted cosiness and comfort. I ran myself a bath and afterwards sat on the settee in my PJs.

I know, I'll read a book, I thought. I hadn't read anything in months – I'd been so busy I hadn't had a chance. However, as soon as I found a book and opened it, my mind began to churn. I thought of Jimmy tucked up in his cot at Jess and Darren's new flat. They'd been in there just over a week now, and I wondered how they were getting on. Then I thought of Lily at home with her mum. I wondered how she was feeling and if she was missing us.

Suddenly the words on the page started to blur in front of me and tears streamed down my face. They were tears of happiness as well as sadness. I felt I'd fought so hard for Jess and Darren to keep their baby, and they had, so I felt an enormous sense of pride and satisfaction about that. Lily's departure had been more unexpected after so many years, but I was happy for her too. I knew both children had gone to the right places, but my heart still yearned for them. This was the hardest part of fostering – the letting go and moving on. But I had no choice. It's my job, and when a child leaves I have to pick myself up and move forward.

However long a child had been with me, all I could hope was that in some little way I'd had an impact on their future and that perhaps they'd remember me. I knew Jimmy wouldn't – he was too young – but Jess and Darren would, and hopefully Lily too.

Suddenly my mobile rang, disturbing my train of thought. It was Vicky.

'I'm ringing to see how you're doing,' she said.

'Oh, I'm just having a good old sob,' I laughed.

'Good for you,' she said. 'You can't beat a good cry to make it all better. Do you want me to come round?'

'Don't be daft,' I told her. 'I'm a snivelling, snotty mess lying on the settee in my pyjamas. Believe me, you don't want to see this.'

My foster carer friends like Vicky and Anne were so important to me and such a good support as they knew exactly how I felt. We'd all experienced children leaving and that huge sense of loss.

'I think it all hit home tonight,' I told her. 'I didn't really have the chance to process saying goodbye to Jimmy because I was so focused on Lily leaving.

'But now she's gone too, and I'm sitting in an empty house and reality has kicked in.'

There was no doubt about it – no matter how long I'd been doing this job, two goodbyes in two weeks had really taken it out of me. I felt their loss like a physical pain, and I knew it was going to take me a long time to get over them both leaving.

NINETEEN

A Family at Last

It was one of those unseasonably warm autumn days, but as usual I'd misjudged the weather and was sweating cobs as I dashed round the house in a jumper and thick black trousers.

'Louisa, please could you wrap Jimmy's present for me?' I shouted from upstairs. 'Otherwise we're going to be late.'

'Yes,' she yelled. 'I'm doing it now.'

I quickly wrote out a birthday card for him and stuck down the envelope. I couldn't believe he was a year old already.

Jess and Darren had been in their new flat for six weeks. We'd chatted on the phone regularly, although I'd only been to visit them once in that time. I felt that after all the drama of the assessment centre, they needed some time on their own as a family without me interfering. Meanwhile I'd been enjoying a little break from fostering. Mentally I felt like I'd needed a bit of a gap between children after Jimmy and Lily had left. I'd done a couple of short respite placements here and there and had caught up on some training courses. As of this week, I was back on the available list with my agency so

I had that nice feeling of anticipation knowing that a placement could come up any day. I finally felt ready for it now, and I was excited by the idea of welcoming a new child or children into my home.

To celebrate Jimmy's birthday, Jess and Darren were having a little party at their flat. I was really pleased to have been invited along with Louisa and Lily, and her mum Jane was coming too. I rushed downstairs. Louisa had kindly wrapped his present for me – a plastic Fisher Price garage and some cars that were normally a big hit with babies of Jimmy's age.

'Right,' I said, picking up my car keys. 'Let's get going.'

On the way there we stopped to pick up Lily and Jane. Lily was doing really well. She seemed happy living with her mum, and she still came to us once a week after school for her tea like we'd promised.

'Jess and Darren will be so pleased to see you,' I told her. 'And their new flat isn't very far from your new house.'

'I can't wait to see Darren.' She smiled. 'And baby Jimmy.'

Darren had proved to be a really good, positive male role model for Lily, which was exactly what she needed after her father.

When we got to the flat and knocked at the door, Jess answered it with a smiling Jimmy in her arms. He was wearing denim dungarees with a little short-sleeved checked shirt.

'Oh my goodness, look at him,' I said. 'He looks so grown-up. Come here, little man.'

'You go to Maggie,' said Jess, passing him into my arms.

Much to my delight, he seemed happy to come to me and gave me a big smile.

'He still recognises us,' said Louisa.

It was lovely to have a cuddle with him after not seeing him for a few weeks, but after a while he started to get restless and wriggly.

'Mam-mam-ma,' he babbled.

'Oh look, he's saying Mama,' laughed Lily.

'Yeah, he likes saying that,' said Jess. 'Especially at five o'clock in the morning when he's wide awake and stood up in his cot.

'I can't wait for him to learn to say Dada, then Daz can get up to him.'

I put Jimmy down on the floor and to my amazement, he pulled himself back up to a standing position using my leg and took a few wobbly steps towards Jess.

'Oh, he's walking!' I said.

'Yeah, he started a couple of weeks ago,' said Jess proudly. 'He's still a bit shaky but he's into everything now.'

'Clever boy, Jimmy,' I told him.

Jess made us all a cup of tea and I was amazed as I looked around the living room. It looked a lot less empty and more homely, and I noticed the chimney breast had been wallpapered.

'I love your flowery wallpaper,' I said.

'Yeah, Daz did that,' said Jess. 'There was a roll of it on sale at Wilko's, so I got it cheap.'

'I put it up, although the flowers ain't my choice,' he said.

Jess also showed me the cushions she'd got from a charity shop and a lamp one of her neighbours had given her.

'You'll meet Karen from next door if she comes round later,' she said. 'She's got two little kiddies, and the youngest is a bit older than Jimmy.'

'That's great that you're making friends, love,' I said.

'The people are actually all right,' she told me.

I was so proud of Jess and Darren. They'd really started to build themselves a proper home and a life in the new place.

They'd put on a little party tea for us all with ham sandwiches and crisps, sausage rolls and cheese triangles and there was a chocolate birthday cake.

'I didn't make it or nothing,' said Jess.

'That doesn't matter,' I told her. 'It all looks lovely.'

They'd put balloons up and Jess had made paper crowns for everyone. She'd written Jimmy's name on his and he wore it while he sat in his high chair. She'd made a real effort, and my heart swelled with pride.

'Daz, tell Maggie your good news,' Jess said.

'I got a job,' he said proudly.

'That's wonderful,' I said. 'Where are you working?'

'Only at Morrison's,' he said. 'But it's regular hours.'

'And he gets a discount on our shopping, so it's really handy,' Jess added.

Jess told me how the worker from the family centre had been round to see them once a week.

'She asked us a few questions and had a cup of tea but she didn't stay long,' said Jess.

'I think she thought we was doing OK,' said Darren.

'You're doing more than OK,' I told them. 'You're doing brilliantly. You shouldn't be worried by her visits at all. She's not checking up on you, she's there to help you.'

'Jess was paranoid,' said Darren. 'She spent hours cleaning the house to impress her, and Jimmy was all dressed up like he was off out for the night.'

'I'm scared,' she said. 'I don't want Social Services to get involved with us again. I still have nightmares about them taking Jimmy away.'

'There is honestly nothing to worry about,' I tried to re-assure them.

The flat was clean and tidy and Jimmy was happy and healthy. I could tell they'd really listened to all the things they'd learnt at the assessment centre. There were plastic storage boxes full of toys in the living room and a pile of picture books for him to pick up and look at. Jess told me she'd even had a go at painting with him, which was admirable with a baby of that age who would just make a massive mess. When I went to the loo, I noticed there was a stair gate on the kitchen door to stop Jimmy going in, and in the bathroom the bath was full of bath toys. They were doing all they could to play with him, stimulate him and keep him safe.

We spent the afternoon eating and playing games. Jess had done a little pass the parcel so we had a game of that – although I'm not sure Jimmy had a clue what was going on. Lily and the rest of us enjoyed it, though! Then we spent the rest of the time opening presents. Lily loved helping Jimmy rip the wrapping paper off, and Jess read each of his cards out loud and showed Jimmy the picture on the front.

It was getting late, and we were all about to leave when I saw Jess giving Darren a nudge about something.

'Before you all go, there's something me and Jess wanted to tell you,' he said.

His cheeks went all flushed and he looked really embarrassed.

'The thing is, we're, er, getting married.'

Jess suddenly looked as embarrassed as he did.

'That's brilliant,' I said. 'I'm so happy for you both.'

'Can I be your bridesmaid?' Louisa asked.

'And me,' piped up Lily.

'We ain't gonna do it just yet,' said Darren. 'We need to save up, so we'll probably wait until Jess is eighteen.'

'He bought me a ring when he got his first wage.' Jess smiled. 'I didn't know he was gonna do it. He just went down Argos and then when he got home he got Jimmy to give the box to me.'

She opened a drawer and got out a sweet little gold ring.

'I didn't want to wear it until we'd told you all,' she said. 'It's only a cubic zirconia but Daz says one day he'll save up enough to swap it for a diamond.'

'Well, I think it's lovely,' I said.

We all oohed and ahhed a little bit longer over Jess's ring, but it was getting late and Jane needed to get Lily home to bed and Louisa had some college work to do. I went to collect our coats from the bedroom where we'd piled them on the bed. Jess came in as I was getting them together.

'Before you go, Maggie, I wanted to say thank you,' she said. 'We ain't had the chance to say it before, but me and Daz are dead grateful to you for what you did for us.

'We probably wouldn't have Jimmy now if it wasn't for you. When everyone else was telling us we was bad parents and trying to take our baby off us, you still believed in us and stood up for us.

'We ain't never going to forget that,' she said. 'Thanks to you, we didn't have to give up our baby. I couldn't have coped if we'd had to do that.'

'It was a pleasure, sweetheart,' I told her. 'But this is down to you and Darren. You did all the hard work. You had your moments, but when you needed to, you pulled your socks up and showed everyone you could be good parents.

'And look at you now,' I said. 'You've got a gorgeous little boy, a lovely flat, you've got engaged and you're making a life for yourselves. I'm really proud of you.'

'Ta, Maggie,' she said, giving me a hug.

'I'll see you soon,' I told her, giving her a kiss on the top of her head.

As I drove Louisa back to our house, I felt all warm and fuzzy. It had been lovely to see Jess and Darren so genuinely happy and content. They might only have been teenagers, but they really cared about each other and looked after one another and now they were a proper family, just like they'd always wanted. Jimmy was well loved and safe and he was growing up in a home with two loving, caring parents. Something neither Jess nor Darren had ever had in their own lives. Through sheer hard work and determination, they'd broken the vicious circle of their pasts.

'It was lovely today, wasn't it?' I said to Louisa.

'Yeah, Jimmy's really cute, and I really liked Jess's ring,' she replied.

As I pulled up into my driveway, I felt my mobile vibrating in my bag.

'One minute, Louisa,' I said, turning the engine off. 'I'd better get this.'

When I glanced at the number, I realised it was Becky, my supervising social worker from the agency.

'Maggie, sorry to bother you at the weekend but I've got a placement I thought you might be interested in,' she said.

I felt that familiar crackle of excitement and intrigue that I always got when I was about to get details of a new child.

'Becky, I'm really interested but I'm just getting out of the car,' I told her. 'Can I call you back when I'm in the house?'

'Of course,' she said. 'But if you could ring me back as soon as you can I'd appreciate it as it's fairly urgent. We need to give Social Services a quick answer on this one.'

I put the phone down and Louisa looked at me questioningly.

'What was all that about?' she asked.

'It was my fostering agency ringing with details about a new placement,' I told her.

'Great,' she said. 'Did they say how old they were, and if it was a boy or a girl? It would be nice to get another baby, wouldn't it, and it's good practice for my course.'

'Slow down, Louisa,' I said. 'I've got to ring her back, so I don't know any of the details yet.'

But as I walked into the house, the one thing I knew for sure was that I couldn't wait to find out.

Epilogue

You don't get many happy endings in fostering, so it's always lovely when things work out. Thankfully, in the cases of Jimmy and Lily they genuinely did. I kept in touch with Jess and Darren for several years. When Jess turned eighteen, they got married. It was a quick service at a register office and then we all went for lunch at the local pub. It was a lovely afternoon – Jimmy made a very cute page boy and Lily and Louisa were bridesmaids. Jess was four months pregnant at their wedding, and they went on to have a daughter called Sarah-Jayne.

The flat was too small for them by then, so they ended up moving away when Darren found a new job in a different town. After that, we slowly lost touch. I was busy with my fostering and I think, if truth be told, as Jimmy got older Jess and Darren wanted to forget that part of their lives. They didn't want reminding that Jimmy had been in care for the first seven months of his life – their family had moved on. Jimmy will be a teenager now, and I suspect that he doesn't know that he was ever in foster care and lived in a family assessment centre for a few months. That's what Jess and Darren have decided, and to be honest, does it matter? What matters is that he has two parents who love him and each other. It's given me a great deal of satisfaction to tell you Jess and Darren's story because it reminded me of why you should always stand up for what you believe in. Yes, they were typical teenagers who'd both had unsettled childhoods, and although the odds were stacked against them, they were in a committed relationship. They genuinely loved and supported each other and they were each other's family. I always believed in them as parents, and thankfully they proved me right.

Fostering Jess taught me many things. That family history is important, but a negative family history shouldn't automatically mean that your own parenting isn't going to be good. In the twenty-odd years that I've been a foster carer, I've had over twenty mother-and-baby placements, but Jess was the only one of them who was in a stable relationship and stayed with her partner. Out of all those placements, I'm proud to say all my teenage mums have kept their babies and none was put up for adoption, and that's a record I hope I keep. As well as teaching them to parent, teenage mums often need to be parented themselves. Their love for their baby is there – they just need to be given the confidence to realise that they can cope, they can be a good mum.

As for Lily, I'm pleased to say that things worked out brilliantly with her mum. She's at university now, and wants to be a nurse. Her mum Jane got married again a few years later and Lily's got two stepbrothers. She still comes round for tea when she's back for the holidays. Again, her story is proof that people can change. Eventually her mum was able to escape her abusive relationship and prove her commitment to win her daughter back. It just took time and patience.

Acknowledgements

Thank you to my children, Tess, Pete and Sam, who I'd not met when Jimmy, Lily and Louisa came into my home but who are such a big part of my fostering today. To my wide circle of fostering friends – you know who you are! Your support and your laughter are valued. To my friend Andrew B. for your continued encouragement and care. Thanks also to Heather Bishop, who spent many hours listening and who enabled this story to be told, and to my literary agent Rowan Lawton and my editor, Anna Valentine at Trapeze, for giving me the opportunity to share these stories.

To contact
Maggie Hartley:

EMAIL
maggie.hartley@orionbooks.co.uk

OR GO TO
facebook.com/maggiehartleyauthor

Also by
MAGGIE HARTLEY

Out now in eBook

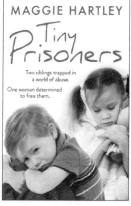

Out now in eBook

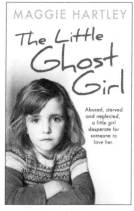

Out now in eBook
and paperback

Out now in eBook

TRAPEZE

COMING SOON

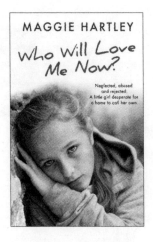

TRAPEZE